Improve Your Grammar

Mark Harrison

Vanessa Jakeman

Ken Paterson

palgrave

Palgrave Study Skills

Business Degree Success
Career Skills
Cite Them Right (8th edn)
Critical Thinking Skills (2nd edn)
e-Learning Skills (2nd edn)
The Exam Skills Handbook (2nd edn)
Great Ways to Learn Anatomy and Physiology
How to Begin Studying English Literature (3rd edn)
How to Manage Your Distance and Open Learning
   Course
How to Manage Your Postgraduate Course
How to Study Foreign Languages
How to Study Linguistics (2nd edn)
How to Use Your Reading in Your Essays
How to Write Better Essays (2nd edn)
How to Write Your Undergraduate Dissertation
Information Skills
The International Student Handbook
IT Skills for Successful Study
The Mature Student's Guide to Writing (3rd edn)
The Mature Student's Handbook
The Palgrave Student Planner
Practical Criticism
Presentation Skills for Students (2nd edn)

The Principles of Writing in Psychology
Professional writing (2nd edn)
Researching Online
Skills for Success (2nd edn)
The Student's Guide to Writing (3rd edn)
Study Skills Connected
Study Skills for International Postgraduates
The Study Skills Handbook (3rd edn)
Study Skills for Speakers of English as a Second
   Language
Studying History (3rd edn)
Studying Law (3rd edn)
Studying Modern Drama (2nd edn)
Studying Psychology (2nd edn)
Teaching Study Skills and Supporting Learning
The Undergraduate Research Handbook
The Work-Based Learning Student Handbook
Work Placements – A Survival Guide for Students
Write it Right (2nd edn)
Writing for Engineers (3rd edn)
Writing for Law
Writing for Nursing and Midwifery Students
   (2nd edn)
You2Uni

Pocket Study Skills

14 Days to Exam Success
Blogs, Wikis, Podcasts and More
Brilliant Writing Tips for Students
Completing Your PhD
Doing Research
Getting Critical
Planning Your Essay
Planning Your PhD
Reading and Making Notes

Referencing and Understanding Plagiarism
Reflective Writing
Report Writing
Science Study Skills
Studying with Dyslexia
Success in Groupwork
Time Management
Writing for University

Palgrave Research Skills

Authoring a PhD
The Foundations of Research (2nd edn)
The Good Supervisor (2nd edn)
The Postgraduate Research Handbook (2nd edn)
Structuring Your Research Thesis

For a complete listing of all our titles in this area please visit www.palgrave.com/studyskills

The authors would like to dedicate this book to Morgan Terry.

First published 2012 by
PALGRAVE MACMILLAN

Palgrave Macmillan in the UK is an imprint of Macmillan Publishers Limited, registered in England, company number 785998, of Houndmills, Basingstoke, Hampshire RG21 6XS.

Palgrave Macmillan in the US is a division of St Martin's Press LLC, 175 Fifth Avenue, New York, NY 10010.

Palgrave Macmillan is the global academic imprint of the above companies and has companies and representatives throughout the world.

Palgrave® and Macmillan® are registered trademarks in the United States, the United Kingdom, Europe and other countries.

ISBN: 978–0–230–36053–2

This book is printed on paper suitable for recycling and made from fully managed and sustained forest sources. Logging, pulping and manufacturing processes are expected to conform to the environmental regulations of the country of origin.

A catalogue record for this book is available from the British Library.

A catalog record for this book is available from the Library of Congress.

10 9 8 7 6 5 4 3 2 1
21 20 19 18 17 16 15 14 13 12

Printed in China

Contents

- on no account / under no circumstances / at no time / in no way (*At no time did anyone consider the repercussions of this action.*)
- not since/ not until /only when (*Not until / Only when the economy improved did their popularity begin to rise.*)
- no matter how/what/who, etc. (*No matter how hard they tried, they could not improve the economy.*)

▶ Key punctuation

▶ Connections within sentences

▶ **Producing good sentences**

▶ Features of writing

Introduction

What is *Improve Your Grammar*?

Improve Your Grammar is a study and practice book for students attending or planning to attend a UK university. It concentrates on the specific areas of grammar and coherence where students frequently make mistakes, and deals with these in a straightforward, accessible way.

The units feature:

- clear, jargon-free explanations;
- a consistent focus on key grammar and coherence areas;
- examples of typical student errors, with corrections;
- tips and key advice;
- a realistic academic context across a range of subject areas;
- easy-to-use practice exercises, with answers.

What are the book's aims?

Improve Your Grammar aims to:

- correct students' grammatical mistakes;
- encourage students to write in an appropriate academic style;
- extend students' range of expression;
- help students to break out of bad habits;

and thereby **improve overall performance** in their subject areas.

What kind of problems does it deal with?

Improve Your Grammar addresses common problems experienced by a large number of students, such as:

- writing sentences that are grammatically incomplete;
- using commas, semi-colons and inverted commas incorrectly;
- confusing *it's* and *its* and *who's* and *whose*;
- using incorrect verb forms;
- failing to connect sentences in an appropriate way, e.g. using *however* and *therefore*;
- making spelling mistakes;
- writing long and confusing sentences;
- writing in an informal or simplistic style.

How is the book organised?

Improve Your Grammar is divided into **60 units**, grouped in sections covering:

- grammar terminology;
- key grammatical areas;
- punctuation;
- ways of connecting sentences;
- step-by-step guides to producing good sentences;
- key features of academic writing;
- vocabulary and spelling.

An important feature of the book is that the contents are presented in **double-page spreads**, making it easy to navigate through the book and to find particular points to consult.

The **first part** of each unit explains the area being covered as simply as possible, with examples of mistakes and how to correct them.

Key information is highlighted in **Writing Tip** boxes, explaining how the unit is relevant to academic work; **Danger Zone** boxes, highlighting very common problem areas; **Rules** boxes, laying down practices that must be followed; and **Remember!** boxes providing essential notes.

The **second part** contains carefully focused practice exercises with answers, allowing users to check their understanding immediately.

Within each section, the units build on each other to cover the principal areas that are essential for students. 'Connections within sentences', for example, contains a series of four linked units focusing on the language required for 'contrasting', 'adding' and describing 'causes' and 'results'.

How should the book be used?

The book has been designed to be as flexible as possible, and may be used both for self-study and in the classroom.

Users should begin with the first two units, which explain key grammatical terms that are used throughout the book.

Units can then be followed in the order in which they appear, providing a comprehensive course of study, or consulted according to need by means of the table of contents or the index.

1 Parts of speech

In grammar, there are different types of word and phrase, which are called **parts of speech** (a misleading term, as it refers to language in any form, spoken or written).

Nouns

- A noun is a word used for a thing or person:
  book, tutor
- Many nouns can be singular or plural:
  source, sources
- Some nouns are called 'uncountable' because they cannot be used in a plural form:
  education, health

Verbs

- A verb is a word used for an action or state:
  write, think
- A verb **tense** is the form of a verb used for the present, the past or the future:
  wrote, will write, was thinking, has given
  ◗ See **4** *Correct tense formation*.
- An **auxiliary** is a form of the verbs 'to be' or 'to have' that is used to create some verb tenses:
  has given, **was** thinking
  An auxiliary is also used for forming negative verbs:
  did not happen, **are not** working
  and questions:
  did it happen? **have** they seen it?
- A **modal** verb is a verb that goes with another verb to express various ideas or shades of meaning.
  Modal verbs are: **may, might, can, could, should, must, ought to, would, will, shall**
  should happen, would not have happened, might be changing
  ◗ See **6** *Modal verbs*.
- A **participle** is a form of a verb used in various verb tenses.
  A **present participle** ends with **-ing**:
  am think**ing**, was work**ing**
  A **regular past participle** ends with **-ed** or **-d**:
  research → had research**ed**, announce → have announce**d**
  Some past participles are **irregular**:
  give → have **given**, think → had **thought**, run → was **run**
  ◗ See **34** *Participles*.

- An **infinitive** is 'to + verb':
  to improve, to conclude
- A **gerund** is a form of a verb ending with -ing:
  start **improving**, therefore **concluding**
  ◗ See **13** *Gerunds and infinitives*.

Adjectives

- An adjective describes the appearance or nature of something:
  long, difficult
- An adjective goes together with a noun:
  a **difficult** question
- A **possessive adjective** indicates that something belongs to or is connected with someone or something:
  my, your, its, his, her, our, their

Adverbs

- An adverb describes how something happens or is done:
  quickly, carefully
- An adverb goes together with a verb:
  think **carefully**
- An adverb can also go with an adjective:
  really beautiful
  ◗ See **50** *Adjectives and adverbs*.

Prepositions

- A preposition is a word or phrase such as:
  at, of, in, on, for, off, out of, from, by, with
- Prepositions are used in many ways, for example in connection with time (on Tuesday), place (in paragraph 2), movement (out of the door), and also in many phrases (off duty, in common)
- Prepositions are used after verbs, nouns and adjectives to form phrases with particular meanings:
  look at a report, take an **interest in**, feel **proud of**
  ◗ See **51** and **52** *Using prepositions*.

Pronouns

- A pronoun is a word that is used instead of a noun or name to refer to people and things.

- Most pronouns are called **personal pronouns**, and they are in various categories:
  subject pronouns → I, you, he, she, it, we, they
  object pronouns → me, you, him, her, it, us, them
  possessive pronouns → mine, yours, its, ours, theirs
- Other words can also be used as pronouns, for example this, that, these, those
  ▸ See **31** *Using pronouns correctly,* and **32** *Avoiding repetition of words.*

Articles

- Articles are the words **a/an** and **the**, used before nouns:
  a review, **an** essay, **the** course
  ▸ See **14** *Articles.*

Linking Words and Phrases

- Words and phrases that join parts of sentences together are sometimes called **conjunctions**, **connectives** or **linkers**.
  Examples of linking words and phrases are:
  and, but, or

  because (of), as, since, due to, as a result (of), therefore, so, so that

  when, while, until, as soon as, once

  if, unless, as long as, provided that, even if

  as well as, in addition (to), furthermore

  although, even though, despite, however, nevertheless, whereas
  ▸ See **26, 27, 28** and **29** *Linking.*

Exercises

1 List the words used in the sentences below according to their parts of speech.

The course provides a useful qualification and graduates regularly find positions in a variety of professions. Full details are available on our website. In addition, we operate an advice service so that prospective students can quickly get clear answers to their queries.

nouns: ....

....

verbs: ....

adjectives: ....

adverbs: ....

prepositions: ....

articles: ....

pronouns: ....

linking words/phrases: ....

2 Match the underlined words with the verb forms A–G.

1 When you have <u>completed</u> the application form, send it to the address below.
2 Your personal statement <u>should</u> include any information relevant to your application.
3 It is important <u>to study</u> the entry requirements carefully.
4 If you are <u>considering</u> this course, go to page 23 for more information.
5 Applications <u>must</u> be received before the closing date.
6 Our students enjoy <u>relaxing</u> in the leisure facilities on campus.
7 Overseas students <u>do</u> not have to fill in this section.
8 We <u>have organised</u> a number of open days for prospective students.

A tense
B auxiliary
C modal
D present participle

E past participle
F infinitive
G gerund

2 Parts of a sentence

A sentence is a group of words that has a clear meaning on its own. It begins with a capital letter and ends with a full stop. A sentence can be short or long.

> **Writing Tip**
>
> If any part of a sentence is grammatically incorrect, or if something that should be there is missing, it will not be considered acceptable in a piece of academic work.

Subject + verb (+ object)

- A sentence must have a **subject** and a **verb** that is connected with it.
- A sentence may also have an **object** after the verb.

▶ **Look at these short, simple sentences:**

Subject — verb
This university is very popular.

Subject — verb — object of verb
This university attracts students from all over the world.

Clauses

- A sentence contains one or more clauses. It must have a main clause.
- A clause is a group of words that may not have a complete meaning on their own.
- In a longer sentence, a clause is one of the building blocks of that sentence, each clause adding to the overall meaning of the sentence.

1 Main clause

- Every sentence has to have a main clause.
- A main clause contains a **subject** and a **verb** and makes sense on its own.
- A sentence may consist only of a main clause:

Subject — verb — two objects linked by 'and'
The university has 600 undergraduates and 300 postgraduate students.

2 Co-ordinated clauses

- A sentence may consist of two main clauses that make sense on their own, linked by a simple conjunction, such as *and, but, so,* etc.
- This is called a **compound sentence**:

1st main clause — conjunction
The university has 600 undergraduates and 300 postgraduate students, ↓ and

2nd main clause
it has a high reputation for its research.

3 Other clauses

- A sentence may consist of a main clause and one or more other clauses which are not main clauses, such as participle clauses or relative clauses.
- The underlined parts of these sentences are clauses. They could not be presented separately as sentences as they do not make sense on their own.
- Clauses may follow one after the other:

participle clause — main clause
Founded in 1922, the university has 600 undergraduates and 300 postgraduate students.

♦ See **34** *Participles*.

- or a clause may be within another clause:

relative clause

The university, <u>which was founded in 1922,</u> has 600 undergraduates and 300 postgraduate students.

◗ See **15** *Relative clauses.*

- A sentence that contains two or more clauses is called a **complex sentence.**
- Clauses are normally separated by commas.

The department underwent reforms which, although they took a while to take effect, proved successful.

This sentence has three clauses:

the main clause → 'The department underwent reforms'

another clause → 'which proved successful.'

another clause → 'although they took a while to take effect'.

- Here are some more examples of how clauses can be used in correctly constructed sentences. In each example, 'the department was expanded' is the main clause.
- A main clause does not have to begin a sentence:

Because so many people were applying for its courses, the department was expanded.

- A clause that is not a main clause does not have to have a verb:

As a result of an increase in applications, the department was expanded.

In this sentence, the other clause has a subject (an increase) but no verb.

- A clause that is not a main clause does not have to have a subject:

To meet demand, the department was expanded.

In this sentence, the other clause has a verb (meet) but no subject.

- A subject or object may be a pronoun:

Owing to an increase in applications to the department, it was expanded.

In this sentence the pronoun 'it' is used as the subject of the main clause.

> 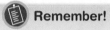 **Remember!**
>
> If you write something that consists of any of the clauses in (3) above **but does not have a main clause**, it is not a real sentence.

Exercises

1 Which of these is NOT a sentence, and why?

    a. The education system in Britain has changed many times in the last hundred years.

    b. Education, one of the biggest issues in British society for a very long time.

    c. Critics considered the 11-plus exam to be an unfair way of deciding the futures of children.

    d. Admissions policies vary from school to school.

2 Identify the subject, main verb and object in each of these sentences.

    1 At some schools, pupils can take the International Baccalaureate.

    2 When they first opened in the 1950s, many people welcomed comprehensive schools as a big improvement in education.

    3 Selective schools usually require candidates to take an entrance exam.

3 Underline the main clause in each of these sentences.

    1 Students applying for university places have to complete the application process, which includes a personal statement.

    2 The three categories of state schools during the 1960s were grammar, comprehensive and secondary modern.

    3 In the 1990s, when polytechnics changed their name and became universities, the overall number of applications for higher education places rose sharply.

4 How many clauses are there in these sentences?

    1 The system for the funding of higher education, which has changed several times over the past few decades, is a major issue in the UK, affecting a great many families.

    2 British universities, because of their high reputation, have long attracted overseas students and these students have become an important source of revenue.

    3 In order to attract students who otherwise may not have gone to a university at all, the variety of courses on offer at British universities has greatly increased over the last two decades.

3   Singular/plural subjects & verbs

A **singular subject** must have a **singular verb**:

↓   ↓

One member of the panel   **was** opposed to the proposal.

A **plural subject** must have a   **plural verb:**

↓   ↓

Most members of the panel   **were** in favour of the proposal.

Some members of the panel   ~~was~~ **were** very enthusiastic about the proposal.

> 💡 **Writing Tip**
>
> Making sure that a verb is correctly singular or plural is an essential part of producing a grammatically correct sentence. You need to pay careful attention to the subject of a verb to avoid making a mistake.

▶ **Look at these incorrect and correct sentences from essays on theories of education and the reasons for the mistakes.**

Why has the mistake been made?

One of the main issues surrounding classrooms from the point of view of teachers are discipline. ❌

→ The word 'issues' is plural but the subject of the verb is 'One' and so the verb must be singular. The sentence is about one issue, 'discipline'.

↓

One of the main issues surrounding classrooms from the point of view of teachers **is** discipline. ✔

Everybody in the teaching profession are in agreement that this is a highly effective way to maximise the potential of all children. ❌

→ Although 'everybody, everyone, nobody, and no one' refer to more than one person, they are grammatically singular words and so must be used with singular verbs.

↓

Everybody in the teaching profession **is** in agreement that this is a highly effective way to maximise the potential of all children. ✔

A very good example of the kind of approaches that work in these situations are pairwork activities. ❌

→ The phrase 'pairwork activities' is plural, but it is not the subject of the verb. The subject is the singular 'example'.

↓

A very good example of the kind of approaches that work in these situations **is** pairwork activities. ✔

This is one of the many problems that has affected the teaching profession for many decades. ❌

→ Although the sentence begins with the singular 'This is', the subject of the verb 'affected' is the plural 'problems'.

↓

This is one of the many **problems** that **have** affected the teaching profession for many decades. ✔

The different ability levels of children in a single class obviously has a big effect on the method a teacher chooses to use. ❌

→ The words 'ability' and 'class' are singular but the subject of the verb is the plural 'levels'.

↓

The different ability **levels** of children in a single class obviously **have** a big effect on the method a teacher chooses to use. ✔

Group nouns

- Group nouns may not end with 's' or 'es' but they still have a plural meaning as they refer to a large number of people or things.
  Words like **police, government, class, crowd, team, public, audience, press, family, community, population** and **staff** are examples of group nouns.
- If the word is used to refer to the group as a single unit, use a singular verb:
  A child's **family has** a huge influence on his or her education.
  The teacher reported that the **class was** very well-behaved.
- If the word is used to refer to the various people in the group, use a plural verb:
  The **child's family were** not all living in the same house.
  The **class were** from different cultural and economic backgrounds.
- Note that 'police' is always used with a plural verb:
  The **police** regularly **visit** the school to give talks to the pupils.

 Remember!

In a complex sentence a verb can be a long way from its subject and it is easy to get confused about whether it should be singular or plural. Always check back to ensure that you have used a correctly singular or plural verb form.

Numbers

- Use a singular verb with '**the** number of' and a plural verb with '**a** (small/large) number of':
  The number of teachers taking career breaks **has** risen significantly in the last three years.
  A number of head teachers **are** paid advisers to other schools in their area.
- With fractions, percentages and proportions, the verb agrees with the noun nearest to it:

⚠ Danger Zone
Is a noun singular or plural?

Some plural nouns do not end with 's' (e.g. people, children, men, women) but they are plural and require a plural verb:
There are many **people** in the teaching profession who ~~takes~~ **take** the view that this is the best approach.
Academic subjects that end with 's' (e.g. politics, economics) are singular but when the same word is used with a different meaning not referring to academic study, a plural verb is used:
Economics is an optional subject on the curriculum. ✔
The **economics** of this proposal **make** it impractical. ✔

During the summer programme, half/50 per cent of the school **day is** devoted to sports.
Three-quarters/75 per cent/The majority of the **schools** in the area **have** reported a decline in bullying.
- Note that 'the average' is used with a singular verb:
  The average age of the children participating in the project **is** seven.

Exercises

1 Decide whether the underlined verbs in these sentences are correct or not.

1 The government <u>is</u> considering various options for reforming the system.
2 Secure parking is one of several issues that <u>has</u> to be addressed urgently by planners.
3 Problems that affect both residents and businesses in the area <u>includes</u> traffic congestion.
4 Noise pollution is something that a great many people <u>is</u> affected by.
5 This is typical of the developments that most <u>concern</u> environmentalists today.
6 A common result of management initiatives affecting staff in these ways <u>is</u> industrial disputes.
7 This is among the repercussions that <u>is</u> seldom foreseen by any expert.

2 Choose the correct verb form.

1 Everybody in those professions with experience of current developments .... (*thinks/think*) that reform is essential.
2 The maintenance costs of a piece of equipment produced to that specification .... (*tends/tend*) to be very high.
3 Figures indicate that a quarter of UK households now .... (*suffers/suffer*) from fuel poverty.
4 Some media commentators suggested that the police .... (*was/were*) responsible for the leak.
5 The number of schools reporting a decrease in truancy .... (*has/have*) doubled over the last five years.
6 The politics that .... (*surrounds/surround*) this issue make it a very controversial one.
7 He was among the members of parliament who .... (*was/were*) elected in 2011.

4 Correct tense formation

A verb **tense** is the form of a verb which relates to the time when something happens.

For example, there are different tenses for **present** actions: ⟶

> **Present Continuous** for ongoing actions in the present.
>
> ↓
>
> New research **is changing** current thinking. (= now)

 Writing Tip

Using correct verb tenses relies on an understanding of the time reference(s) in every sentence that you write. Accurate tense formation and use are essential and basic aspects of any piece of writing.

> Research **is** vital for the development of counselling practice. (= always)
>
> ↑
>
> **Present Simple** for present states, truths, etc.

Past simple (I did it) and present perfect (I have done it)

▶ **Look at these incorrect sentences from essays on psychology and consider why the underlined verb tenses are wrong.**

Since the 1980s, an increasing number of people in the UK <u>did</u> courses enabling them to practise as counsellors. ✗
Two decades ago, the number of professionals involved in counselling <u>has grown</u> suddenly. ✗

What's wrong: The wrong tenses are used. The choice of tense must match the time that is being referred to in the sentence.

Rules

Use the **past simple** tense if you are referring to a time in the past and talking about something that was completed at that time:
<u>During the first session</u>, the counsellor **asked** a number of general questions. ✓

Use the **present perfect** tense when the time mentioned includes the past and the present:
<u>In the sessions so far</u>, the counsellor **has tried** to identify the exact nature of the problem. ✓

• Here are the incorrect sentences above with the correct tenses:

<u>Since the 1980s</u>, an increasing number of people in the UK **have done** courses enabling them to practise as counsellors.	→	The phrase 'Since the 1980s' refers to a period of time that includes the present, so the **present perfect** is required.
<u>Two decades ago</u>, the number of professionals involved in counselling **grew** suddenly.	→	The phrase 'Two decades ago' refers to the past only, so the **past simple** is required.

Remember!

If you are talking about something that is fully in the past, use the past simple. If you are talking about something that covers both the past and the present, use the present perfect.

Continuous verb tenses

<u>At that time</u>, counsellors **were dealing with** the situation for the first time.	→	The **past continuous** (*was/were* + *-ing*) describes an action or situation continuing at a particular point in the past.

The training course for counsellors **has been running** for two years now.	→ The **present perfect continuous** (*have/has + been + -ing*) is used for something continuing for a period of time starting in the past and still happening now.

Past perfect simple (I had done) and past perfect continuous (I had been doing)

By 1990, the number of trained counsellors **had risen** significantly.	→ The **past perfect** (*had + past participle*) refers to something that happened before or until a particular time in the past.
Prior to this date, many people **had been suffering** on their own with mental health problems.	→ The **past perfect continuous** (*had been + -ing*) is used for something continuing for a period of time before a particular point in the past.

 Danger Zone

We was / He done it

Many people use incorrect forms of basic verb tenses when they are talking but you must not do this when you are writing. Two very common incorrect forms are:

We was talking about .... ❌   They was right when they said ... ❌

- Remember that 'we' and 'they' are plural and they are followed by 'were', not 'was'.
  We were talking about .... ✔   **They were right** when they said ... ✔

  He done it very well. ❌
- This verb form does not exist. There are two possible correct forms:
  He did it very well. ✔ (if you are talking about something completely in the past);
  He has done it very well. ✔ (if you are talking about something with a connection to the present).

Exercises

1 Decide whether the underlined verb tenses are correct or not.

1 In recent times, new evidence pointing to the real causes of this problem <u>has emerged</u>.
2 It was at that point that the benefits of radical reform of the system <u>have become</u> apparent.
3 Since then, numerous studies <u>supported</u> this theory.
4 At the start of this decade, nobody <u>foresaw</u> these developments.
5 In the last few years, people <u>have started</u> to question this approach.
6 Back then, few experts <u>have realised</u> the importance of these findings.

2 Complete this paragraph by circling the correct verb tenses.

One of the main appeals of any new technology is the novelty value that it (1) *has/is having*. When mobile phones, for example, (2) *was/were* new and expensive, owners (3) *liked/were liking* to display them to impress others. After they (4) *have been using/had been using* them for a while, however, the novelty (5) *wore/has worn* off. In the mid 1990s, not many people (6) *were owning/owned* one, but by the early 2000s, most people (7) *had bought/bought* one and (8) *were using/have been using* it regularly. Nowadays, they (9) *became/have become* part of everyday life and newer, more exciting developments (10) *were attracting/have been attracting* the attention of the general public.

5   Using more than one verb tense

In July last year, an experiment **was set up**, in which different groups of participants who **had not previously met**, and **did not receive** any preparation, **answered** questions while they **were dealing** with a number of different tasks.

> ### 💡 Writing Tip
> You will often need to use more than one verb tense in a single sentence or paragraph and sometimes you will need to use the same verb tense more than once. This is particularly true when you are writing reports, describing results or presenting a sequence of events.

▶ **Look at the verb tenses in bold in these incorrect sentences from reports on research.**

1   Incorrectly mixing past and present tenses

The groups went into separate rooms so that they **can't** hear each other. ❌

What's wrong: The first verb is in the past and so the second verb must also be in the past.
The groups **went** into separate rooms so that they **couldn't** hear each other. ✔

If, however, you want to describe how this experiment works in general, you could use the present for both verbs:
In this experiment, the groups **go** into separate rooms so that they **can't** hear each other.

What you must not do is mix the past and present in this way.

2   Describing one past action that followed another past action

Once they **completed** the tasks in one room, the groups went into another room. ❌

What's wrong: The sentence describes something in the past that happens before another action can happen. The past perfect must be used for the first action.
Once they **had completed** the tasks in one room, the groups **went** into another room. ✔

Time words and phrases such as 'When', 'As soon as' and 'After' are followed by the past perfect in this context.
When/As soon as/After they **had completed** the first task, the group **went on** to do the second task.

3   Misusing the present perfect tense

The results showed that the second group **have done** the tasks better than the first. ❌

What's wrong: The present perfect (have done) cannot be used to talk about something that is completely in the past. Because 'had done' happened before 'showed' (first they did the task, then the results showed something), the past perfect (had done) can be used.
Because both things happened completely in the past, the past simple (did) can also be used.
The results **showed** that the second group **had done/did** the task better than the first. ✔

4   Describing something that is generally true

People who adopt that approach to the task **are always doing** it well. ❌

What's wrong: The first verb is talking about something that is generally true and the second verb should be in the same tense because it is also talking about something generally true. The present continuous (are doing) is incorrect because it refers only to the present moment or period of time.
People who **adopt** that approach to the task always **do** it well. ✔

5 Reporting speech

Researchers told all the participants that they **did** very well. ✖

What's wrong: When you are reporting what someone said in the past, you need to change the tense of the verb that person used when they spoke. In this case, the speaker said 'You did very well' or 'You've done very well'.

Researchers **told** all the subjects that they **had done** very well. ✔

Reporting information

The following tense changes are made when reporting information:

		The researchers reported that ….
The results **look** remarkably consistent.	→	the results **looked** remarkably consistent.
We **are analysing** the results.	→	they **were analysing** the results.
The experiments **were** successful.	→	the experiments **had been** successful.
We **have formed** certain conclusions.	→	they **had formed** certain conclusions.
The results **will** have important effects.	→	the results **would** have important effects.

> **❗ Danger Zone**
> ### Mistakes when reporting
>
> In spoken language, an incorrect tense for reporting may not matter but in academic work it is inappropriate.
>
> The researchers claimed that their study means that common beliefs on the subject are wrong. ✖
> The researchers **claimed** that their study **meant** that common beliefs on the subject **were** wrong. ✔

Exercises

1 Decide whether the underlined verb tenses in these sentences are correct or not, and correct those which are not.

1 It was clear that the situation <u>could not continue</u> and that something had to be done as a matter of urgency.
2 When the researchers <u>analysed</u> all the evidence, they formed their conclusions.
3 They presented the data so that a non-expert <u>can understand</u> it.
4 The poem was a new direction for him because <u>he had not written</u> in that style before.
5 He wrote about subjects that still <u>have</u> relevance for people in this day and age.
6 After people <u>came</u> to terms with the shock of this event, they began to adapt to the new circumstances.

2 Complete the reported statements.

1 The report stated: 'Fish are returning to the river now that it is unpolluted.'
The reported stated that ....

2 'I will stay in office until the board has appointed a successor,' he announced.
He announced that ....

3 A spokesman said: 'We are investigating the problem but have not found the cause yet.'
A spokesman said that ....

4 An official statement declared: 'The talks were successful and we hope to sign an agreement.'
An official statement declared that ....

5 A government report predicted: 'Until exports rise, economic growth will not return.'
A government report predicted that ....

6 'I cannot comment because I do not know the details of this case,' the spokeswoman replied.
The spokeswoman replied that ....

6 Modal verbs

Modal verbs are used before other verbs to express various meanings; **can, could, may, might, must, need, ought to** and **should** are modal verbs.

> 💡 **Writing Tip**
>
> Modal verbs add to, modify or change the meaning of verbs in important ways. In academic writing they can play a fundamental role in expressing attitude and point of view. There are a number of key areas where you need to get them right.

Problems with past forms

► Look at these sentences from an essay on fashion management and the mistakes in them.

1 Using 'of' instead of 'have'

The organisers should of been able to predict the press reaction to the show. ❌

What's wrong: In spoken English *have* may sound like *of*, but it is never correct to write *of* as part of a past modal form.

The organisers should **have** been able to predict the press reaction to the show. ✅

> ❗ **Danger Zone**
>
> **Should of/ Would of/ Could of/ Must of**
>
> Never use 'of' after any modal verb. When talking about the past, use 'have':
>
> In a different economic climate, sales of the new designs would ~~of~~ **have** been better.
>
> Without that piece of good fortune, she might not ~~of~~ **have** become such a well-known designer.

2 Incorrect use of 'could'

After extensive negotiations, Select Design could make an exclusive agreement with Topshop. ❌

What's wrong: You cannot use *could* for a specific achievement in the past. Instead, you need to use *was/ were able to* or *managed to* or *succeeded in*.

After extensive negotiations, Select Design **was able to** make/ **managed to** make/ **succeeded in** making an exclusive agreement with Topshop. ✅

3 did not need to /need not have

My Frock Ltd did not need to go bankrupt if they had restricted their business to the UK. ❌

What's wrong: *Did not need to* + verb is used for things that **did not** happen (because they were not necessary). The clients **did not need to** secure a loan in order to set up The Suit Company as they had sufficient savings. ✅ *Need not have* + past participle is used for things that **did** happen (but they were not necessary). My Frock Ltd **need not have gone** bankrupt if they had restricted their business to the UK. ✅

4 Incorrect use of 'must not have'

The designer handbags on sale at £25 each must not have been genuine. ❌

What's wrong: To express the opposite of *must have been* (meaning 'this is the logical conclusion'), you need to use *cannot* or *could not have been*, not *must not have been*.

The designer handbags on sale at £25 each **cannot/could not have been** genuine. ✅

should and must

● You can use **should** to express two meanings:
  1 'It's a good idea'
    Products **should** be attractive as well as functional.
    With this meaning, *should* is weaker than *must*.

2 'It's likely'

The exhibition **should** attract a wide audience, because the drawings have never been seen in the UK until now. With this meaning, *should* is stronger than *may/might/could*.

- You can use **must** to express two meanings:

1 'It is necessary'

Designs for public buildings **must** take into account the needs of all the users.

The negative forms **must not** and **do not have to** have different meanings:

Visitors to the gallery ~~do not have to~~ **must not** touch the exhibits. (= it's not allowed)

Visitors to the gallery ~~must not~~ **do not have to** pay, but can make a donation. (= it's optional)

The past form is **had to**:

The exhibition was so popular that timed tickets **had to** be issued.

2 'This is the logical conclusion'

Some of the missing ceramics **must be** in private collections.

Bacon **must have destroyed** some of his early paintings.

The negative forms are **cannot + verb** for the present and **cannot/could not have + past participle** for the past:

Stevens argues that estimations of the cost of restoring the building **cannot** be correct.

Vince Green **could not have known** that Stella Law was working on exactly the same designs.

(*See 4 Incorrect use of 'must not have' above.*)

ought to

Ought to is more formal than *should*, but means exactly the same. Note the forms:

present: **ought to / ought not to + verb**

Theatre designs **ought not to** distract the audience from the meaning of the play.

past: **ought to have / ought not to have + past participle**

The reproductions in the catalogue **ought to have been** larger.

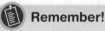 **Remember!**

Modal verbs, like other verbs, can have continuous and passive forms:

We **may be seeing** a revival of interest in the techniques used to produce stained-glass windows.

Her paintings **can be studied** from a number of different perspectives.

Exercises

1 Write the correct option in the space.

1 Dress Right managed to save money because they .... (did not need to open/need not have opened) an office in Paris.

2 French Style Ltd .... (must have released/had to release) a statement in March 2010 saying that their factories did not employ workers on twenty-hour shifts.

3 Sue Cape .... (must not/cannot) be the first jeweller to work exclusively in Welsh gold, but she is making a reputation as the most interesting.

4 If he had made a full apology, designer Tom Gott .... (did not need to resign./need not have resigned.)

5 Foster .... (must have been working/must have worked) on the painting when he died, because the half-finished canvas was found in his studio.

6 The new range of cosmetics .... (should/can) sell well next year in Japan, where Jay Kay products have become popular in the teenage market.

2 Correct any sentences that are wrong.

1 Dalio's work in sculpture must not have been a success because she soon turned to painting.

2 From an early age Wender could cut fabric better than his colleagues.

3 With a more attractive design, the product could of become a brand leader.

4 Critics argued that the gallery ought to have not allowed the painting to be sold to a museum.

5 Fortunately, the organisers could save the show by using a back-up generator.

6 The exhibition could have been promoted more effectively.

7 Using the passive

The passive is a verb form. Verbs can be in the 'active' or 'passive' form.

- An **active** verb is used when the subject 'does' the verb:
  The **voters** of Merthyr Tydfil **elected** Keir Hardie as the first Labour Party MP in 1900.
  The subject is '*voters*' and they '*elected*'.
- A **passive** verb is used when the subject does not 'do' the verb:
  Keir Hardie was elected as the first Labour MP by the voters of Merthyr Tydfil in 1900.
  The subject is '*Keir Hardie*' but he did not '*elect*'; someone else – the voters – '*elected*'.
- In the examples above, the passive is more effective because Keir Hardie is the main focus of the sentence, not the voters.

> ### Writing Tip
> The passive helps your reader focus on the important part of your sentence. It is particularly useful when you want to achieve the impersonal style that academic writing sometimes requires.

- There are several reasons for using the passive. Here are some examples:

Sentence		Reason for using the passive
At that time, **reforms** to the voting system **were being brought in** by the new government.	→	The event is more important than the person/people/thing that did it.
Her **application** to become an MP **has been rejected.**	→	The writer does not know who did the action.
The protestors **were** all **sentenced** to six months in prison.	→	It is not worth mentioning who did the action because it is obvious (a judge).
It **is believed** that rebel forces used the internet to plan their campaign.	→	The writer is putting across a view or claim that may not be fact. (*See **Passives with reporting verbs** below.*)

> ### ⋔ Rules
> The passive is made using a form of the verb *be* + past participle (*designed, taken* etc.). Here are examples:
>
> | | |
> |---|---|
> | David Cameron **was elected** to Parliament in 2001. | *active: they elected David Cameron* |
> | A new political party **has been established**. | *active: they have established* |
> | The televising of trials **is** currently **being discussed**. | *active: they are discussing* |
> | The offender **was being taken** to jail when he escaped. | *active: they were taking* |
> | After a ceasefire **had been agreed**, fighting stopped. | *active: they had agreed* |
> | New immigrants **will be given** an English test. | *active: they will give* |
> | A recount **may be held** because the vote was so close. | *active: they may hold a recount* |
> | Sara Kemp hopes **to be re-elected** next year. | *active: hopes voters will re-elect her* |
> | No MP likes **being criticised** by his own party. | *active: likes his own party criticising him* |

▶ **Read this paragraph from an article on the Palace of Westminster and consider why each passive was used.**

The Palace of Westminster comprises the House of Commons and the House of Lords. It **was designed** by Charles Barry in Gothic style, and the foundations **were laid** in 1840. The Palace **was finally completed** more than 30 years later, after a number of delays. In 1987 it **was declared** a 'World Heritage Site' by UNESCO.

▶ **Read these sentences from a student's essay.**

Some citizens were planning a new political party when the backers withdrew their funding.
After the office had released a statement, the minister refused to take further questions. ✗

What's wrong: The passive should be used to make the important information stand out. 'Some citizens' is too vague to mention.

A new political party **was being planned** when the backers withdrew their funding. ✔

The statement is much more important than the official who released it.

After a statement **had been released**, the Minister refused to take further questions. ✔

Passives with reporting verbs

Writers sometimes use passive forms of reporting verbs such as *believe, claim, know, report, say, think, understand.* There are two patterns:

It + be + *believed/said* etc. + that...
It was known that Winston Churchill suffered from short periods of depression.

Noun + be + *believed/said* etc. + present/past/continuous infinitive...
Winston Churchill was known to suffer from short periods of depression.

▶ **Read these sentences from students' essays.**

People think that translation services are costing the European Union more than €1bn a year. ✘
Experts say that economic problems led to their election defeat. ✘

What's wrong: The passive should be used to de-personalise the claims that are being made and give the sentences a more academic tone.

It is thought that translation services are costing the European Union more than €1bn a year. ✔
Translation services are thought to be costing the European Union more than €1bn a year. ✔

It is said that economic problems led to their election defeat. ✔
Economic problems are said to have led to their election defeat. ✔

Exercises

1 Rewrite these sentences, starting with the underlined part.

1 Former American President Jimmy Carter won <u>the Nobel Peace Prize in 2002</u>.
2 MPs will debate <u>the Bill</u> later in the week.
3 A clerk was destroying <u>the documents</u> when the police arrived.
4 The Government might postpone <u>the referendum</u>.
5 Protestors have occupied <u>three government buildings</u>.
6 Rioters had stolen <u>most of the museum's collection</u> by the time the army arrived.

2 Rewrite these sentences in two ways using reporting verbs.

1 Commentators believe that Walter Clark is the Senate's most skilful debater.
   It...
   Walter Clark...
2 A journalist reported that two politicians took bribes for their votes.
   It...
   Two politicians...
3 Officials say that talks are taking place between the two parties.
   It...
   Talks...
4 People think that Che Guevara was executed to avoid the drama of a trial.
   It...
   Che Guevara...

❗ Danger Zone

Overusing the passive

Don't overuse the passive. Both sentences below have an academic tone but the second, active one is better because it places the focus on the essay and keeps the key words 'examine' and 'causes' together.

The causes of economic decline in two previously successful European countries will be examined in the essay. ✘

This essay will examine the causes of economic decline in two previously successful European countries. ✔

8 Direct & indirect questions

A **direct question** is a <u>question</u> that is actually asked:

> What can we conclude from the evidence?

💡 **Writing Tip**

In formal, academic writing, indirect questions are more commonly used than direct questions, although direct questions can be effective at times. It is important to use both types of question correctly.

An **indirect question** is a <u>statement</u> that is based on a direct question that was asked or could be asked.
We must decide what we can conclude from the evidence.
It is not clear whether we can conclude anything from the evidence.

▶ **Read this paragraph from an essay about laws and look at the direct (1) and indirect (2) questions in it. Look at the punctuation too.**

One of the fundamental issues surrounding the introduction of any new law is this: **Is it possible to enforce it?** (1) Lawmakers know that they have to work out **how to ensure that** (2) people adhere to the new law and they have to ask themselves: **What do we need to consider** (1) in order to ensure that this law has a realistic chance of being effective? They need to be absolutely clear as to **how the authorities will enforce** (2) it. With attempts to legislate in connection with the internet, this fundamental issue is particularly pertinent. **How can such legislation work?** (1) There might be general agreement as to **why such laws are required** (2) but enforcement is almost impossible to guarantee.

Direct questions

Some direct questions ask for the answer '**Yes**' or '**No**' → *Is it possible?*
Some direct questions ask for **information** → *What do we need?*

A direct question can be formed with these patterns:
- the verb 'be' + subject:
  Is it possible to enforce it?
- a modal verb (can, should, will etc.) + subject + main verb:
  How **can such legislation work**?
- an auxiliary (do, does, have, had, etc.) + subject + main verb:
  What **do we need** to consider...?

📋 **Remember!**

Put a **question mark** at the end of a direct question.

Put a **colon** before a direct question and begin it with a capital letter if the question is at the end of a sentence.

Indirect questions

Indirect questions do not have the same word order as direct questions – they are not phrased as questions, they are phrased as statements.

Direct question → *Is it possible?*

Indirect question → *They need to know whether it is possible.*

An indirect question can be formed with these patterns:

- question word + subject + verb:
  They need to be absolutely clear as to **how the authorities will enforce** it.
  There might be general agreement as to **why such laws are required** but ...

- question word + 'to' infinitive:
  ... they have to work out **how to ensure** that people ...

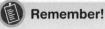

Remember!

Do not put a question mark at the end of an indirect question.

Do not phrase an indirect question in the same way as a direct question.

ⓘ Danger Zone

Incorrect phrasing of indirect questions

An indirect question is a statement, not a question. It uses the same word order for subject, verb, etc. as any other statement:

Research has been carried out to discover <u>what experts regard</u> as the most serious legal issues surrounding the internet. ✔

Research has been carried out to discover what do experts regard as the ... ✘

Exercises

1 Decide whether these indirect questions are written correctly, and correct the ones that are not.

1. It was hard for legislators at the time to foresee what would the effects of this law be.
2. It is instructive to examine why it took so long for the issue to be addressed.
3. Things change and at times it is necessary to ask whether certain laws should be modified to accommodate those changes.
4. Experts need to co-operate in order to determine exactly how can a new law be implemented.
5. Many professionals are still finding out how does the internet affect them from a professional point of view.
6. Creating the law is one thing, but nobody knows how much harder it will be to enforce it.
7. The public should be clear about whether or not have they broken the law.

2 Complete the indirect questions.

1. Why is such a law required?
   We have to ask ourselves ....

2. When did this problem first arise?
   It is hard to be exact about ....

3. What were the origins of this law?
   It would be useful to know ....

4. How quickly can the law be implemented?
   People are asking ....

5. In what areas should we implement this law?
   We have to decide ....

6. What other laws will we need in the future?
   The public is asking ....

7. Have I broken the law?
   People need to know ....

9 Conditionals (If...)

Sentences using if are called **conditionals**.

They always contain two parts: the if clause which expresses the condition, and a clause expressing the result.

If Wiretech plc had invested in new technology, they might have survived the recession.
→ *It did not survive because it did not invest.*

> ### 💡 Writing Tip
>
> Using conditional sentences allows you to link causes with effects, both real and speculative. They are a key part of academic writing.

Conditionals for the past

▶ **Read this incorrect sentence from a business case study.**

If Lyons Brothers would have sold some of their assets, they could have avoided making 20 per cent of their workforce redundant. ✗

What's wrong: In the 'if' clause you need to use the past perfect tense (*had* + past participle).

- Here is the correct version:

If Lyons Brothers **had sold** some of their assets, they could have avoided making 20 per cent of their workforce redundant. ✓

- You can use different modal verbs in the result clause to express different meanings:

may/might/could → a possible result

would → a definite result

If senior managers had wanted to avoid a dispute with the union, they **would have allowed** a longer period for negotiation.

The strike **might not have happened** if senior managers hadn't taken such a hard line in negotiations.

- You can use a present form of a modal verb to talk about a **present result**:

If the strikes had not happened, the company **would be** in a stronger position today.

> ### 📋 Remember!
>
> The 'if' clause can come first or second. If it comes first, you need a comma after it:
>
> If the consortium had paid in dollars, they would have got a discount.
> The consortium would have got a discount if they had paid in dollars.

Variations of the 'if' clause

Even if the product had been re-branded, it would have made a loss.	→ **Whether or not** the product had been re-branded, ...
Had the Government intervened, the shipyard might have remained open.	**If** the Government **had** intervened, ... → *Placing 'had' at the beginning and removing 'if' makes the style more formal.*
If it had not been for... **Had it not been for...** **But for/Without...** the oil leak, BP would have made record profits.	**If** there **had not** been an oil leak, .../ **If** the oil leak **had not** happened, ... → *Note that all four phrases are followed directly by a noun phrase ('the oil leak').*

Conditionals for present and future

- The structure **'if' clause + result** can also be used to write about the **present** and **future**:
  If it **is registered** at Companies House, a business **must** submit an annual financial statement.
  There **will be** few winners if interest rates **rise** dramatically. (NOT 'will rise')
- **Provided that/as long as** can be used instead of *if* when the meaning is 'only if' or 'on condition that':
  Provided that/As long as demand outstrips supply, the price **will** continue to rise.
- **Unless** means 'except if' or 'if .... not' and is used with a **positive verb**:
  Customers will complain **unless** the service **is** improved. (NOT 'is not improved')

Conditionals for speculating

- Using a **past simple** tense in the 'if' clause and a **present modal** verb allows you to speculate:
  If developing countries **controlled** commodity prices, they **could** plan their economies better.
  In formal writing, *were* is preferred in the 'if' clause to the singular form *was*:
  If fast broadband access **were** available on the island, it **would** help local businesses.
  Were to + infinitive and **If it were not for...**, can also be used:
  If the company **were to relocate**, it **could** reduce its energy costs.
  If it were not for its increased export sales, WTC **would** be in financial difficulties.

Exercises

1 Rewrite the sentences using *if* and the modal verbs in brackets.

1 Techgames did not lose their share of the youth market because they did not increase their prices. (would)
   If Techgames ....

2 Bailey Ltd probably failed because they did not use internet marketing. (might)
   Bailey Ltd ....

3 The sales team did not win new orders because they did not attend the trade fair in Barcelona. (could)
   The sales team ....

4 The advertising campaign did not focus on young professionals, and it did not succeed. (would)
   If ....

5 Longgame plc is flourishing today because it diversified five years ago. (would)
   If it ....

2 Complete each gap with <u>two</u> words.

1 .... its highly-skilled workforce, the north-east would not have attracted the new car plant.
2 .... committee carried out a full investigation in 2006, it would have discovered that two substantial bribes had been paid.
3 .... not been for the region's easy access to solar power, business costs would have soared.
4 .... it had cut costs substantially, the company would not have avoided bankruptcy.
5 .... had not been for their inflexible recruitment policy, the Dalkeith factory could have taken advantage of the market in part-time workers.

3 Correct any of the sentences that are wrong by adding or replacing a word.

1 If CEO Barry Cranston were found guilty of insider trading, he would have to stand down.
2 If video links were replace trade fairs, sales teams would lose the vital link with retailers in the places where they live and work.
3 If supermarkets did not sell goods other than foods, they would not be as profitable as they are.
4 If there were not for Goldworth's successful Paris branch, the company would be making a loss.
5 Unless the agreement is signed, it has no validity in law.
6 Provided as it continues to innovate, the company has a bright future.

10   Time words & phrases

yet	still	meanwhile	only	soon	in the process of	any longer

💡 Writing Tip

There are a number of expressions connected with time that are more appropriate in academic writing than the simpler ones used in spoken and informal language.

▶ Read this paragraph from an economics essay and look at the words and phrases in bold that refer to the times when things happen.

At that point, the worst of the economic crisis was **yet to** happen. Countries knew that they could not go on adding to their debt burden **any longer**, but paying down their debt proved to be beyond many of them. Various emergency measures were carried out but these **were to** provide only temporary respite. They dealt with the immediate crisis, **only** to exacerbate the problems later on. **During the course** of the next few years, one crisis followed another. **Meanwhile**, unemployment was rising, as was inflation. **So far**, nothing had worked and the biggest crisis of all was **soon to** follow.

Future time

As well as writing about the 'future in the present', we also write about the 'future in the past'.

have/be + yet/still + infinitive

- used to talk about things that have not happened but might happen in the future:

The full repercussions of the financial crisis haven't been felt yet.	→	The full repercussions of the economic crisis **have/are yet to be felt.**

- used to talk about things that had not happened at a point in the past but perhaps happened later:

These fundamental economic problems still hadn't been addressed.	→	These fundamental economic problems **had/were still to be addressed.**

only/soon + infinitive

- used to talk about an undesirable outcome or something bad that happens next:

The government took drastic action, **only to discover** that the problem was even worse than it seemed.	→	*but it discovered later that …*
Banks **were soon to discover** that the position was even worse than they had feared.	→	*Banks soon discovered that …*

be + infinitive

- used to refer to how something developed later in time:

Inflation **was to become** a major problem, though people did not predict it at the time.	→	*Inflation became …*

prove + infinitive

- used instead of informal expressions such as 'turned out' to talk about the reality after a period of time. All infinitive forms can be used in this structure:

Strict economic policies **proved to be** the only solution.	→	*It became clear that strict economic policies were the only solution.*

on the verge/point of –ing .....

- used instead of the more informal 'be about to' to talk about something likely to happen a short time in the future:

Inflation was **on the point/verge of** reaching a record high at that time.	→	*It was about to reach a record high (perhaps it reached it, perhaps it didn't).*

Periods of time

meanwhile

- for talking about different but connected things happening during the same period of time:
  Credit was/is easily available and both consumer spending and property values were/are rising fast. **Meanwhile**, an economic crisis was/is looming.

during the course of ...

- for referring to a period of time involving a development or developments:
  During the course of this/that decade, economic growth (has) reached unprecedented heights.

in the process of -ing

- for talking about something happening over a period of time in order to achieve an aim:
  The government was/is **in the process of bringing** inflation under control and it was/is already beginning to fall.

any more / any longer / no longer

- for talking about something that happened for a period of time and then stopped happening
- use **any more** and **any longer** with **negative verbs** at the end of a sentence or clause:
  People **could not / cannot rely** on easy credit **any more/any longer**.
- use **no longer** between the two parts of a **positive verb**:
  People realised that they **could no longer rely** on easy credit.

> **! Danger Zone**
>
> **Any more, any longer & no longer**
>
> - **any more** is two words
>   *anymore* ✗
> - use **any longer** with **negative verbs**:
>   They <u>couldn't rely</u> on easy credit **any longer**.
> - **no longer** is **not** used with **negative verbs**:
>   They couldn't no longer rely on easy credit. ✗
>   They couldn't rely on easy credit no longer. ✗

Exercises

1 Rewrite the bracketed parts of each sentence using the word in bold.

1 New laws have been discussed but they (haven't been implemented yet). **are**
2 It is important not to take a hasty decision (and regret it later). **only**
3 Scientists said that they were (about to find a cure for the disease). **verge**
4 The real causes of the disaster (still hadn't emerged). **had**
5 At that time, they were (reforming the system). **process**
6 Later it turned out that this decision (had been a very good one). **proved**
7 He was (about to resign) when the situation suddenly changed. **point**
8 Fortunately, the situation (soon improved). **was**
9 That decision (had unforeseen consequences). **was**

2 Create two sentences out of the following single sentences, using 'meanwhile'.

a. While industrial relations were reaching an all-time low in the 1970s, overseas competitors were flourishing.
b. The country was developing economically and at the same time it was also changing culturally.

3 Decide if these sentences are correct or not, and correct those that are not.

1 The old way of doing things was not relevant anymore.
2 By the 1970s, televisions weren't expensive for most people no longer.
3 They found that their marketing strategy wasn't working any more.
4 By the 1960s, Britain was no longer a colonial power.

11 Emphasising

Emphatic language strengthens a writer's argument.

People need to appreciate that
speeding causes accidents.
→
**What people need to appreciate
is** that speeding causes accidents.

> ### Writing Tip
> Although you often need to be cautious in academic writing, there will
> be other times when your tutor will expect you to express strong and
> confident arguments.

▶ **Read this text and look at the phrases in bold.**

Mass tourism undoubtedly brings problems as well as benefits to newly discovered regions. **Only by examining a key set of issues in detail can we decide** whether a town or region has actually benefited from tourism. A good place to start is the local economy. **What one will notice quite quickly is** the number of new businesses that have emerged since the first influx of visitors. All of these may have brought in new income and created jobs, but **it is their seasonal nature that** distinguishes them from the traditional economy: when the tourists leave, the restaurants and souvenir shops in the main tourist areas – and the streets themselves – go into a kind of hibernation, perhaps for six months on end, during which time nothing happens at all.

- The text illustrates three emphatic structures:

1 Only by + -ing phrase

America needs to encourage drivers to scale down
the size of their cars and reduce their dependence
on oil.
→
**Only by encouraging drivers to scale down
the size of their cars will** America succeed in
reducing its dependence on oil.

NOTE: This structure is normally followed by 'will' or 'can', and the word order changes.

2 What + subject + verb + be

The UK needs a Minister of Transport with a real
sense of vision.
→
What the UK needs is a Minister of Transport
with a real sense of vision.

3 It + is/was + noun + that/who

The tour operator must take responsibility if
package accommodation is at fault.
→
It is the tour operator who must take
responsibility if package accommodation is at
fault.

▶ **Look at these sentences about travel and find a mistake in each one.**

It is the lack of information what makes travellers angry when there are airport delays. ✗
What are passengers looking for is a train service that is punctual and not overcrowded. ✗
Only by acting on consumer feedback travel companies can improve their performance. ✗

What's wrong: There are mistakes in the words used or in word order.

- Here are the correct versions of these sentences:
  It is the lack of information **that** makes travellers angry when there are delays at airports. ✓
  What passengers **are** looking for is a train service that is punctual and not overcrowded. ✓
  Only by acting on consumer feedback **can** travel companies improve their performance. ✓

- Here are some other ways of emphasising:

4 Using a **word + a reflexive pronoun** (*e.g. itself* or *themselves*)

A poorly-performing hotel can only improve if **the management itself** recognises the problems.
The use of itself *emphasises that it is the* management *that needs to accept that there are problems, rather than someone else such as the staff.*

5 Using **emphatic adverbs**

- clearly, obviously, undoubtedly
  Heathrow is **undoubtedly** a major success story, but it has problematic aspects.

- absolutely, completely, entirely, utterly, wholly
  The travel patterns of the general public in the poorest communities of the world are **entirely** different from those in affluent countries.

- indeed
  There are a number of car-sharing schemes in operation in London which are very successful **indeed**.

- quite = 'completely' when used with adjectives such as *certain, different, impossible, sure, true, wrong*
  We can be **quite sure** that there will be protests against the proposed construction.

- *whatsoever* or *at all* with negative statements
  The council made no provision **at all** for car parking.
  Despite complaints from the guests, nothing **whatsoever** was done to improve the catering at the hotel.

> **Remember!**
> Use the emphatic adverbs in this section to emphasise a key point that you want the reader to take special notice of.

▶ **Look back at the paragraph on page 22 and find some examples of 4 and 5.**

Exercises

1 Rewrite these sentences, emphasising the important parts.

1 The one-way system was making the situation worse.
It ....

2 Visitors to Scotland enjoy its magnificent scenery most.
What ....

3 Consumers must purchase local produce to reduce the amount of food transportation.
Only by ....

4 People want easy access to the main tourist sites.
What ....

5 Most passengers seek value for money rather than luxury in an airline operator.
It ....

6 Resorts have to retain their essential character if they want to attract tourism in the long term.
Only by ....

2 Complete this text with the words below.

indeed, whatsoever, entirely, itself, undoubtedly

There is **1** .... a growing trend for independent travelling in its widest sense. This can range from travel agencies assisting customers in their tailor-made arrangements to complex trips planned with no professional input **2** .... Often it is the planning **3** .... that the new breed of traveller enjoys, and the results can prove to be very interesting **4** .... For example, a teacher from Surrey recently chose to spend a month **5** .... alone on an Indonesian island normally inhabited only by parrots and monkeys.

12   Negative expressions & structures

> **Writing Tip**
>
> There are a number of negative expressions that can be very effective in academic writing. They are not commonly used in informal speech but are very appropriate in more formal contexts such as essays. To use these expressions correctly, you need to pay careful attention to the grammatical rules that apply to them.

▶ **Read this paragraph from an essay about politics and look at the negative expressions in bold.**

> This was a particularly difficult period for the government. **No matter** what they did, everything seemed to go wrong. **Neither** their handling of the economy at home **nor** their foreign policies proved effective. **No sooner** had they weathered one storm than another one arrived. **At no time** were they able to get to grips with events, as one crisis after another overwhelmed them. MPs faced a dilemma: they did not want to publicly rebel against the leadership but they could not allow things to continue in this way **either**. **Not since** the leadership battle of 20 years earlier had there been such a key moment in the party's history.

neither ... nor

● used with **positive verbs** (not negative verbs) in various patterns

Neither the public **nor** their own party members **supported** the policy. → neither A nor B + positive verb

The minister **neither spoke** in favour of the policy **nor criticised** it.

→ neither + positive verb + nor + positive verb   ◗ See Danger Zone **33** *Parallel structures.*

Neither did the policy increase the government's popularity **nor did it work** in a practical way.

The policy **did not increase** the government's popularity **nor did it work** in a practical way.

→ neither/nor + auxiliary + subject + verb; use this pattern if you begin a sentence or clause with neither/nor.

negative verb + either

● used after a second negative idea /statement/fact

They decided that it would be unwise to raise taxes and they **did not want** to cut spending **either**.

Other negative expressions and structures

● These expressions are all used to make emphatic or dramatic statements that highlight the importance of a situation, fact or event.   ◗ See also **11** *Emphasising.*

● In most of them, the question pattern is used:

> **Remember!**
>
> Do not use a negative verb with 'neither'. Use 'either' with a negative verb:
>
> They **did not want** to raise taxes and they **did not want** to cut spending **either**. ✔
>
> They did not want to raise taxes and they did not want to cut spending neither. ✘

	auxiliary	subject	verb
	↓	↓	↓
	Did +	you +	lose the election?

no sooner ... than / hardly ... when

● used for talking about one thing happening immediately or very soon after another

No sooner had one crisis passed than another arose.

Hardly had one crisis passed when another arose.

on no account / under no circumstances; at no time; in no way

● used for emphasising negative points

Under no circumstances/On no account could they allow their opponents to know the full facts.

At no time did they seem to be in control of events.

In no way could this be described as a success.

not since; not until /only when; it was not until/only when ... that

● used for referring to important points in time

Not since the recession 20 years earlier **had a government been** so unpopular.

Not until/Only when the economy improved **did their popularity begin** to rise.

It was not until/only when the economy improved **that** their popularity began to rise.

NOTE: This last expression has a 'normal' subject + verb word order.

no matter how/what/who, etc.

- used for saying that one fact makes no difference to another

No matter how hard they tried, they could not improve the economy.

No matter what they did, they could not improve the economy.

NOTE: These expressions are followed by a 'normal' subject + verb word order.

❗ Danger Zone 1

Double negatives

Use a **positive verb** with the negative words **no, no one, nothing,** etc:

They **made no** progress for a couple of years.

The policy **pleased no one**.

They **could do nothing** right as far as the public were concerned.

Use **any, anyone, anything,** etc with a **negative verb**:

They **did not make any** progress ...

The policy **did not please anyone**.

They **could not do anything** right ...

Do not use a negative verb with no, no one, nothing, etc:

They didn't make no progress ... ❌

The policy didn't please no one. ❌

They couldn't do nothing right ... ❌

❗ Danger Zone 2

Confusing use of two negatives

It can be very confusing to use two negative verbs close together in a sentence.

They didn't not support the proposal but they had some reservations about it. ❌

It wasn't a matter that wasn't important but there were other priorities. ❌

To avoid using negative verbs close together, you need to think of alternative ways of phrasing, for example:

They were not opposed to the proposal but they had some reservations about it. ✅

It was a matter of some importance but there were other priorities. ✅

NOTE: If you avoid using contracted forms, you are less likely to make this kind of mistake.

Exercises

1 Decide if the underlined words in these sentences are correct or not and correct those which are not.

1 The new IT systems did not did not improve efficiency nor <u>were they</u> popular with staff.
2 The advantages of this solution were that it would not be difficult to implement and it would not be very expensive <u>neither</u>.
3 Voters listened to the politicians' words and they were neither reassured by them <u>or</u> interested in them.
4 Neither the media <u>nor</u> the public accepted the official version of events.
5 At the time, experts did not see <u>nothing</u> wrong with this theory.
6 It was not a popular policy nor <u>it was</u> a successful one.

2 Rewrite the sentences starting with the words in bold.

1 As soon as people had become accustomed to the situation, it changed. **No sooner**
2 They worked very quickly but they could not keep up with demand. **No matter**
3 She got rid of one reporter but then another one appeared. **Hardly**
4 The policy could not be allowed to fail on any account. **On no account**
5 People did not begin to worry about the economy until inflation started to rise. **It was only when**
6 This has not been considered an important issue until recent times. **Not until**

3 Rewrite these sentences to avoid using two negatives.

1 The policy worked but it wasn't particularly successful.
2 This isn't something that can't be explained fairly easily.
3 Not many voters did not feel that the election result was a foregone conclusion.

13 Gerunds & infinitives

A **gerund** is a verb that ends with **-ing** → keeping

An **infinitive** is **to + verb** → to keep

> **Writing Tip**
>
> Correctly using the -ing or infinitive form of a verb is an essential aspect of grammatical accuracy.

▶ **Read this paragraph from an essay about industrial relations and look at the verb forms in bold.**

At the meeting, senior management and union leaders **discussed implementing** new working practices and scales of pay. They **attempted to reach** agreement on these issues and each side **expected** the other side **to compromise**. However, **finding** solutions to some of the areas of disagreement proved extremely difficult. **To give** everyone an opportunity to consult their colleagues, the meeting was adjourned. When the talks resumed, management **tried to make** the union leaders **see** how important it was to modernise but they remained **opposed to implementing** some of the ideas.

-ing

● Here are some examples of verbs that you might need to use in academic work that are followed by the -ing form of another verb:

deny	justify	avoid/resist/delay	consider/contemplate	imagine	dislike/resent
suggest/recommend/discuss		involve/mean/entail	risk	mention/describe	anticipate

Union representatives **denied causing** the talks to break down.
The management were unable to **justify imposing** unfair terms on the workforce.
It was clear that the proposal would **entail/involve/mean making** 200 people redundant.
Union officials would not **contemplate/consider agreeing** to the terms.
Strikers **described/mentioned being** reluctant to go on strike.

infinitive

● Here are some examples of verbs that you might need to use in academic work that are followed by the infinitive form of another verb:

threaten/demand	refuse/agree/decide/choose	claim/pretend	promise/guarantee/undertake
attempt	fail/manage	plan/intend/aim/mean	wish/want

Workers **demanded to have** longer holidays and **threatened to go** on strike.
After some discussion, they **decided/chose/refused/agreed to accept** the terms.
They **claimed/pretended to represent** the views of the entire workforce.
Both sides **promised/guaranteed/undertook to honour** the agreement.

Verb + object + infinitive

want/expect	encourage/urge/persuade/convince/invite	warn/advise	force/drive/compel/oblige

● These verbs use this pattern:
Union leaders **encouraged/urged/persuaded/convinced** <u>members</u> **to accept** the deal.
Militant union officials **warned/advised** <u>their colleagues</u> **not to accept** the terms.

Note that *force/drive/compel/oblige* are usually used in the passive form:
Employees complained that they **were being forced/compelled/obliged/driven to work** unsocial hours.

Gerund as subject

● You can use a gerund as the subject of a verb: subject   main verb

Persuading the workforce **proved** very difficult.

Infinitive for purpose

- You can use an infinitive to talk about the purpose of an action:

    They made various concessions **to persuade** the workforce to agree.

    To persuade the workforce to agree, they made various concessions.

 Remember!

The verb **make** is followed by an infinitive without 'to':

No amount of persuasion would make the workforce to agree. ✗

No amount of persuasion would **make the workforce agree**. ✓

⚠ Danger Zone

To + ing

There are a few verbs and phrases that use the -ing form after 'to', not the infinitive form:

Managers were not **accustomed/used to listening** to the wishes of the workforce.

Both sides became **resigned/reconciled to compromising** on various issues.

It seemed for a while that they were **close to reaching** an agreement.

They could not **adapt/adjust to working** in those conditions.

Nobody would **admit to being** responsible for the talks breaking down.

Unable to succeed through negotiation, the leaders **resorted to making** threats.

Neither side was **looking forward to meeting** the other.

... accustomed to listen ... ✗   ... admit to be responsible ... ✗

... adapt to work ... ✗   ... looking forward to meet ... ✗

Exercises

1 Complete these sentences with the gerund, infinitive or to + ing form of the verbs in brackets.

  1 They realised that returning to profitability would mean .... (introduce) radical measures and they decided .... (draft) outline plans for this.

  2 They met to discuss .... (restructure) the department and they are now close .... (finalise) the details.

  3 If you feel that you are being obliged .... (implement) decisions that you don't agree with, you tend to resist .... (carry) them out for as long as possible.

  4 The board did not want to risk .... (lose) market share and they were opposed .... (change) their marketing strategy in any radical way.

  5 All departments heads undertook .... (improve) productivity in their departments but they warned management .... (not have) unrealistic expectations of what could be achieved.

  6 Sales figures encouraged them .... (believe) that their strategy was working and so they would not contemplate .... (change) it.

  7 They knew that modernising the company would entail .... (make) some people redundant but they did not anticipate .... (have) to reduce staff numbers so much.

  8 The owners were looking forward .... (increase) the profits over the coming year and the consultants recommended .... (recruit) more staff in order to achieve this.

2 Five of the underlined verb forms in this paragraph are incorrect. Find them and correct them.

One of the major problems of his period as Prime Minister was that he could not admit <u>to make</u> any mistakes. Aides urged him <u>to do</u> so, on the grounds that it would make the public <u>to think</u> differently about him. They told him that the public expected their leaders <u>to show</u> a human side but he refused <u>taking</u> any notice of their advice. He would not consider <u>altering</u> his approach and he denied <u>having</u> an image that the public found off-putting. Accustomed <u>to have</u> his own way, he resented <u>to be</u> told that he needed to make concessions to public opinion. For two more years, he tried to justify <u>continuing</u> in the same old way, but eventually the voters had their say.

3 Change the verbs in brackets into gerunds or infinitives.

  1 (avoid) ..... any future misunderstandings, they signed a written agreement.

  2 (get) ..... funding for the research proved a major obstacle.

  3 It was clear that ..... (find) a suitable location for the new stadium would be a major issue.

  4 Notices were displayed ..... (ensure) that people knew the health and safety regulations.

14 Articles (a/an, the)

The grammatical term for **a/an** and **the** is **articles**: **a/an** → the **indefinite article**; **the** → the **definite article**.

> ### 💡 Writing Tip
>
> Not using articles correctly is a basic error that will give a bad impression of your work. It is essential to use an article when it is required and it is just as essential not to use an article when it is wrong to do so.

▶ **Read this paragraph from an essay on media and look at when articles are used and not used.**

> **The birth** of what is now commonly called **celebrity culture** can be traced to **the 1980s**. Before then, **a famous person** could assume that he or she could maintain some privacy out of **the glare of the media** and without attracting **the attention of the public**. There were **gossip columns** in **newspapers** and of course **scandals** were common but **life** was different for celebrities until the 1980s. During that decade there was **a huge change** in **attitudes towards famous people** and this coincided with **the arrival of** new magazines such as 'Hello'. **The celebrities that they covered** were paid **large sums** to give **readers an insight into** their private lives and **the stories and interviews** in them took **an uncritical view** of their subjects. **The change in attitudes** started here.

Use 'a/an'

- to talk about one of many, but not a particular one: a famous person → any famous person
- when you are using a singular noun for the first time, not referring to someone or something already mentioned: a huge change → the word 'change' is introduced here.

Use 'the'

- When there can only be one:
  the birth of / the arrival of
- When you are referring to a specific one or ones and saying which one or ones:
  the glare of the media / the attention of the public / the celebrities that they covered → *which glare, whose attention, which celebrities are all explained in the phrases*
- Before something that has been mentioned earlier:
  The change in attitudes started here. → *the change previously mentioned*
- Before a group noun:
  the media / the public *(but not 'the society')*
  ♦ See also **3** *Singular/plural subjects and verbs.*
- Before a decade or century:
  the 1980s

> ### 📋 Remember!
>
> Use 'the' when you are specifying or explaining which one/ones but don't use 'the' when you are generalising or talking about abstract concepts.

Don't use 'the'

- With plural nouns when you are generalising rather than specifying which ones:
  gossip columns in newspapers / scandals were common → *particular gossip columns, newspapers and scandals are not specified*
- With singular nouns that describe abstract concepts or ideas rather than particular examples of these:
  life was different → *this refers to the abstract concept of 'life', not a particular life*
- With plural nouns when you have not mentioned them previously:
  attitudes towards famous people / large sums → *these do not refer to any attitudes or sums previously mentioned*
- With plural nouns when it is understood which ones you are talking about:
  readers → *this can only refer to readers of the magazines being discussed*
  NOTE: Some well-known phrases include an article, e.g. an insight into, the majority of

Using 'the' when it should not be used

▶ **Look at these incorrect sentences:**

Nowadays the celebrities have become a major conversation topic because they are in the news. ✖

→

These magazines show images of the wealth and happiness. ✖

→

Some people say that these magazines have the articles that are worthless. ✖

→

What's wrong?

This sentence refers to 'celebrities' in general, not specific ones, so 'the' must not be used.

'the' should be left out because 'wealth' and 'happiness' are abstract concepts.

'articles' have not previously been mentioned and it is obvious that it means articles in the magazines, so 'the' should be left out.

- However, all these sentences could be correctly written with 'the' if the noun is followed by a phrase explaining or specifying which one or ones are being described.
- Here are correct sentences both without and with 'the':

Nowadays, celebrities have become a major conversation topic because they are in the news.
Nowadays, people often have conversations about **the celebrities who are in the news.** ✔

These magazines show images of wealth and happiness that fascinate people.
The wealth and happiness shown in these magazines fascinates people. ✔

Some people say that these magazines have articles that are worthless.
Some people say that **the articles in these magazines** are worthless. ✔

> **❗ Danger Zone**
>
> **Words beginning with 'h'**
>
> If 'h' is pronounced when you say the word, use 'a':
> a happy society
> a habitat
>
> If 'h' is not pronounced when you say the word, use 'an':
> an honest man   a honest man ✖
> an hour   a hour ✖

Exercises

1 Decide whether these sentences are correct or not and correct those that are not.

1 For most parents, the education is one of the biggest sources of a concern with regard to their children.
2 There was a huge difference between the incomes of people living in the same street.
3 Despite spending the large amounts of money, the government did not manage to achieve its targets for the health care.
4 It has been argued that people now have the higher expectations of the life and that this can cause them an unhappiness.

2 Complete these sentences with the correct article or no article.

1 In 1955, he travelled to India and, on his return, he wrote ..... emotional account of ..... experiences he had had on ..... journey.
2 Towards ..... end of ..... 20th century, ... lives of many people in ..... developed countries were transformed by ..... arrival of ..... computer technology.
3 Suddenly, ... entire industry changed and ..... new approach was required to ..... whole area of marketing.
4 There wasn't ..... obvious solution to ..... problem and ..... opinions varied as to what ..... best course of action was.
5 Many people claim in ..... surveys that ..... job satisfaction is more important than ..... high salary.

3 Find six incorrect uses of 'the' in this paragraph and underline them.

It became clear that the further research was required and the two people who carried this out were faced with the problem of how best to do it. After the discussions, they decided that the focus of the research should be the attitudes to the happiness because they wanted to focus on the effect of the increased prosperity on the modern society. Having decided on this, they set out to find the kind of subjects that would best suit their purpose.

15 Relative clauses: who, which, that, etc.

Clauses that start with who, which, that, etc. are called **relative clauses**.

The words who, which and that are called **relative pronouns**.

💡 **Writing Tip**

Relative clauses allow you to define and add information to what you are saying. Used correctly, they can be a very effective writing tool.

🌱 Rules

There are two types of relative clause:

1 A defining clause that gives information that is **essential** to the sentence:
   Brunel was the engineer <u>**who** first realised the potential of wider tracks for higher-speed trains.</u>
   Without the relative clause, the sentence does not make sense.

2 A non-defining clause that gives useful, additional information:
   Optical fibres, <u>**which** have a much higher capacity than copper cables</u>, have revolutionised the telecommunications industry.
   Without the relative clause, the sentence still makes sense.
   NOTE: In the second type, there is a comma both before and after the clause.

• In the first type, 'that' can be used instead of 'which' or 'who':
   The integrated circuit was the key development **which/that** led to the personal computer.
• In the second type you cannot replace 'which' or 'who' with 'that'.

▶ **Look at these sentences about inventions and discoveries and try to find the mistakes in each one.**

A patent is a legal document, which prevents others from exploiting an invention for a fixed period. ❌
Grace Hopper who was born in 1906 in New York developed the idea of machine-independent programming languages for computers. ❌
In 2006, Pluto was reclassified as a 'dwarf planet' by the International Astronomical Union, that is a recognised body of professional astronomers. ❌

What's wrong: There are mistakes in punctuation and in the use of relative pronouns.

• Here are the correct versions of these sentences:
A patent is a legal document which prevents others from exploiting an invention for a fixed period. ✔
The information about a patent is essential to the sentence, so there should not be a comma before 'which'.
Grace Hopper, who was born in 1906 in New York, developed the idea of machine-independent programming languages for computers. ✔
The information about Hopper's birth is not essential so the relative clause 'who...New York' needs to be separated by commas.
In 2006, Pluto was reclassified as a 'dwarf planet' by the International Astronomical Union, which is a recognised body of professional astronomers. ✔
This is an example of the second type of relative clause, so 'which' cannot become 'that'.

📋 Remember!

In a relative clause, *which* can sometimes refer to a whole 'idea', not just a noun.

The geneticist Steve Jones discussed his hope of finding cures for a number of serious illnesses, **which** inspired many of those who heard his lecture.

Here 'which' = 'his hope of finding cures for a number of serious illnesses'.

whom

- Use **whom after prepositions** such as *by, for, from, to, with,* etc.
  Stephen Hawking is the physicist **with whom** the general public is most familiar.

whose and which

- **whose + noun** shows 'possession' for people and things such as companies, committees etc.
  The Anti-Vivisection League is an organisation **whose opposition** to experiments on animals is well known.
  whose → the Anti-Vivisection League's
  NOTE: Do not confuse **whose** and **who's**.   ◈ See **57** *Commonly confused words.*
- When writing about things, you can sometimes use **of which** instead.
  A European conference on embryo research, **whose details/the details of which** have not yet been announced, is likely to be held in Milan next year.
- You can also use other prepositions with **which**; for example, the expressions **way in which** and **extent to which** are common.
  Most commentators agree that **the way in which** engineering is perceived by young people may have to change before we see an increase in its popularity as a university subject.
- You can use **where** instead of **in which** with the words *place, area, situation* etc.
  The treatment of anexoria nervosa and bulimia is an area **in which/where** there is a great deal of disagreement.

> ### ❗ Danger Zone
> **Whom or who?**
>
> Don't forget to use 'whom' not 'who' after a preposition.
> There were three people **for whom** the discovery was beneficial. ✔
> There were three people for who the discovery was beneficial. ✖
> Note: 'whom' is not simply a more sophisticated form of 'who' and cannot be used generally instead of 'who'.

Exercises

1 Tick the correct sentences.

  1 Much research has been conducted into schizophrenia, that causes chronic behavioural problems.
  2 Cox argues that it was the Universal Turing Machine of the 1930s that led the way to digital computing.
  3 Newton and Einstein are considered to be the scientists to who modern physics owes the greatest debt.
  4 Water which is regarded as evidence of life may have existed relatively recently on the surface of Mars.
  5 Dr Abel chairs a panel whose views on stem cell research are regularly reported in the media.

2 Rewrite these sentences to include the information in brackets.

  1 A number of questions were asked about the equipment. (It was used in the experiment.)
  2 The Jodrell Bank Observatory has played an important part in researching meteors, pulsars and quasars. (It was established in 1945.)
  3 John Nash made some of the key early insights into modern game theory. (This led to his being co-awarded the Nobel Prize in 1994.)
  4 Michael Faraday was a scientist. (His research into magnetic fields gained him his reputation.)
  5 During the lecture the audience were introduced to Margaret Simons. (She had first identified two of the species of spider being discussed.)

3 Fill each gap in these texts with a preposition + 'which', 'whose' or 'whom'.

  1 The engineer and entrepreneur James Dyson has been critical of the UK business environment for the way .... it has prioritised selling and marketing over design and manufacturing.
  2 Scientists are the people .... we turn for the cures for all our illnesses, yet many complain about the extent .... research funding ignores lesser-known diseases.
  3 Louis Pasteur is the French chemist .... the process of 'pasteurisation' is named.

16 Comparing & contrasting

Adjective: good; **comparative adjective**: better; **superlative adjective**: best / worst

Adverb: quickly; **comparative adverb**: more quickly; **superlative adverb**: most quickly

> ### 💡 Writing Tip
>
> You will often need to compare and contrast ideas, policies, organisations, technologies, etc. in your writing. Make sure you know the rules for forming comparative adjectives and adverbs and that you can vary your use of comparative forms and structures.

> ### Rules
>
> - Add -er/-est to **one-syllable** adjectives (adj.) and adverbs (adv.):
>   (adj.) low → lower → lowest; (adv.) soon → sooner → soonest;
>   but 'double' the consonant when there is a single vowel + single consonant:
>   big → bigger → biggest; hot → hotter → hottest.
>
> - Add -er/-est to **two-syllable** adjectives ending in -ow, -er (and -y, but change the -y to -i):
>   narrow → narrower → narrowest; clever → cleverer → cleverest; noisy → noisier → noisiest.
>
> - Use more/most or less/least with adverbs and all other adjectives of **two syllables or more**:
>   (adv.) efficiently → more/less efficiently → most/least efficiently;
>   (adj.) famous → more/less famous → most/least famous.
>
> - Note the exceptions:
>   (adj.) good/(adv.) well → better → best; (adj.) bad/(adv.) badly → worse → worst;
>   far → further → furthest (farther/farthest is also possible, but less common).

Two main structures

1. **comparative adjective/adverb + than**
   Manufacturing costs are **higher** in southern China **than** in the poorer inland regions.
   For the third successive year Causeway plc is trading **less successfully than** its competitors.
2. **(not) as + adjective/adverb + as**
   Research shows that start-up companies in the manufacturing sector are **not** performing **as well as** new businesses in the service sector.
   Note where a/an are placed in the phrase as + adjective + noun:
   Despite a poor first quarter, 2010 was **not** as difficult **a** year for most SMEs as 2009.

▶ **Look at these sentences from case studies of companies and try to find the mistakes:**

In 2008, Senia produced a new mobile phone that was more thin than their existing models. ✗
Land was cheap, but skilled labour was not as easy to find by the coast than in the cities. ✗
The company realised that coal supplies could be delivered more cheap by road than by rail. ✗
The worse year for the factory in terms of production was 2006, when there were two strikes. ✗

What's wrong: The comparative structures and forms are incorrect.

- Here are the correct versions of these sentences:
  In 2008, Senia produced a new mobile phone that was **thinner** than their existing models. ✓
  Land was cheap, but skilled labour was not as easy to find by the coast **as** in the cities. ✓
  The company realised that coal supplies could be delivered more **cheaply** by road than by rail. ✓
  The **worst** year for the factory in terms of production was 2006, when there were two strikes. ✓

You can make comparisons with expectations, or with the past.

Finding a new location for the factory proved to be **more difficult** than the senior management team had predicted.

The construction of smaller flats, often for the buy-to-let market, is **not as profitable as** it was ten years ago.

❗ **Danger Zone**

1 NOT 'more easier'

Comparatives must be correctly formed. If 'er' has been added to an adjective, it is wrong to use 'more' as well. If 'more' is being used with an adverb, the adverb should have the normal ending.

Manufacturing products can be **easier than** selling them. ✔

The manufacturing team met their deadlines **more easily than** they had expected. ✔

Establishing a customer base was more easier than the team had expected. ✖

2 less/fewer

Remember to use 'fewer' with plural words.

fewer customers ✔

less money ✔

We have less customers on Sunday than on Saturday. ✖

Exercises

1 Rewrite the sentences using the word(s) in brackets.

1 Staff development opportunities are not as important to factory employees as clear lines of communication. (*less...than*)
   Staff development opportunities ....

2 Raw materials cannot be transported as quickly by road as by train. (*more...than*)
   Raw materials ....

3 British businesses are spending less than European companies on product design, according to recent studies. (*not...as....as*)
   British businesses ....

4 The replacements from Germany were not as heavy as the French engines. (*...than*)
   The French engines..

5 Export results and import figures are equally impressive this year. (*as...as*)
   Export results ....

6 The safety systems were not checked as regularly as they should have been. (*less...than*)
   The safety systems ....

2 Correct the sentences that are wrong.

1 Kenton was asked to design a vehicle that would operate in the wetest conditions.

2 It was not as effective system as the manufacturers had hoped.

3 Smalley plc realised that their profit margins would be slimmer in the UK than abroad.

4 Generally speaking, there are less opportunities for apprenticeships these days.

5 If the parts are cooled by water, the process can be completed more sooner.

6 Grayson UK's factory in Berwick is the furthest from London.

7 Some of the world's most desirable cars are criticised for also being the less fuel-efficient.

8 The workforce agreed that a shift system was the most safe way of working.

17 Describing similarities & differences

▶ Read this short text on river pollution, noting the words and phrases that are used to describe similarities and differences.

Although the Danube is **more than twice as long as** the Rhine, **both are similar in that** they have their sources in central Europe. The Danube, however, **unlike** the westward-flowing Rhine, travels east through countries that have not been able to invest in expensive water treatment plants. While the Rhine Action Programme has ensured that the river is **80 per cent cleaner** than it was 20 years ago, the Danube Pollution Reduction Programme, **in contrast**, has been far less successful.

Modifying adjectives and adverbs

- For structures with a comparative adjective/adverb (+ *than*), you can use *much, a great deal, far,* or the opposites *slightly, a little, marginally* – or percentages (as in the text above):
  Earthquake damage is **much greater** in areas where housing has been poorly constructed.
  The tornado that struck New York was **marginally less powerful** than predicted.
- For structures with as (*...as*), you can use *just* or *almost, nearly* or *not quite, not nearly*:
  Gabions (cages of boulders) are **just as effective as** seawalls in preventing erosion, and **not nearly** as expensive.
- For superlatives, you can use *almost, one/some of* or the opposite *by far*:
  Vindija is a cave in Croatia that contains **some of the best** preserved Neanderthal remains in the world.

Numbers

- For numbers, use *twice + as (many)...as* or *three/four times + as (many)...as* or *than* – and you can be even more precise by adding *at least, nearly, more than* or *exactly*:
  In Ireland, where there are **nearly twice as many** sheep as people, any change in agricultural policy is likely to have far-reaching consequences.
  Fertile soil is being lost in Europe **more than 50 times faster** than it can be replaced through natural processes.

Words/phrases for similarity

- **alike, similar to, like, to resemble**
  Leopards and panthers are **alike/similar in that** both of these big cats are strong swimmers.
  Lake Huron **is similar to/is like/resembles** Lake Michigan **in terms of/as regards/with respect to** surface area and maximum depth.
- **in the same way/similarly**
  Ecologists have argued that heavy logging is destroying large tracts of the Amazon Rainforest. **In the same way/Similarly**, urban clearance is reducing West Africa's rainforest.
- **similarity/in common**
  The main **similarity between** America and Australia is the large coastal population.
  All cultivated crops **have** several characteristics **in common/have several similarities**.

Words/phrases for contrast

- **dissimilar to, different from, unlike, to differ**

  The Grey Whale **is dissimilar to/is different from/differs from/is unlike** other baleen whales in that it feeds by filtering small organisms from the mud of shallow seas.

- **in contrast to/contrary to/unlike**

  'Flying squirrels', **in contrast to/contrary to/unlike** bats, glide rather than actually fly.

⚠ Danger Zone

On the contrary / in contrast/on the other hand

On the contrary means that the opposite is true, but *in contrast* and *on the other hand* link two contrasting but equally true situations:

The future of the koala is by no means secure. **On the contrary**, habitat loss and unbanisation may well require the Australian Government to designate these mammals as a 'threatened' species. ✓

A tornado 'watch alert' tells the public that the conditions which cause tornados are present. A 'warning alert', **on the other hand/in contrast**, is issued when an eyewitness has actually made a sighting. ✓

Coastal erosion in the area has not worsened over the past decade. *On the other hand*, coastlines have remained intact. ✗

Exercises

1 Choose the correct word/phrase from the brackets to complete each sentence.

1 A new study of the state of the world's biodiversity suggests that species are dying out .... (*by far/twice/far*) faster than scientists had previously thought.

2 On account of their moveable thumbs, chimpanzees are .... (*just/ exactly/slightly*) as able as humans to grasp and hold on to objects.

3 Some studies have indicated that Antarctic ice is melting .... (*more/twice/by far*) as quickly as ten years ago.

4 The kori bustard is .... (*one of/far/at least*) the heaviest birds in the world capable of flight.

5 According to UK Kennel Club registrations, the Labrador Retriever is .... (*at least/by far/ slightly*) four times more popular than the King Charles Spaniel.

2 Complete the sentences by putting a word/phrase from the box in each space.

differ	in common	similarly	in contrast	on the contrary

1 The survival of these villages depends on the stock of local tuna. ...., secondary industries nearby, such as canning, rely on regular supplies of this fish.

2 Summers on the coast .... from the tropical inland area in that they are windy and cool.

3 Discoveries of shale gas are not met with universal approval; ...., many commentators fear the environmental damage that extraction will bring.

4 The soil in both of these regions has a number of features ....

5 .... to Brown's optimistic study, Fisher notes a worrying decline in the numbers of wildflower species in the region.

3 Use the language from this unit, and the table below, to write a short text comparing some of the breeding behaviour of female lions and tigers.

	Lions	Tigers
Gestation period	100 days	100 days
Average litter size	4	3
Average time mothers spend nursing cubs	11 months	24 months
Age of sexual maturity in cubs	40 months	40 months

18 Using noun phrases

The community → a noun

Recently established traffic-calming systems in the community → a noun phrase

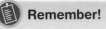
▶ **Compare these two sentences on the subject of local politics.**

If community groups <u>get together to buy</u> land, they <u>can prevent</u> it from <u>being developed</u> in a way that they <u>find</u> undesirable. → This sentence is built around the underlined verbs.

The joint purchase of land by community groups leads to **the prevention of** what they regard as **undesirable development**. → This sentence is built around the noun phrases in bold. It has a more **academic style** than the first sentence.

- Here are some ways of creating sentences based on nouns.
  1 **using the noun form of verbs or adjectives:**
    Councillors criticised the way in which newspapers **covered** the local elections.
    Councillors criticised **newspaper coverage of** the local elections.
    Several councillors wondered how **reliable** the traffic statistics were.
    Several councillors questioned **the reliability of** the traffic statistics.
  2 **using a noun with the same meaning as a whole phrase:**
    A number of people doubted that the recycling scheme **could be kept going for a long time**.
    There were doubts about **the sustainability of** the recycling scheme.
    Local residents opposed the way in which the council **put** the new planning laws **into practice**.
    There was local opposition to **the council's implementation of** the new planning laws.
  3 **using the -ing form of a verb as a noun:**
    If the town hall's facade were **cleaned**, it could become a more attractive local feature.
    The cleaning of the town hall's facade could make it a more attractive local feature.
- ▸ See **53** *Using longer words* and **54** *Using single words for impact*.

> **Remember!**
> Using nouns and noun phrases makes it possible to put the important idea (e.g. *the joint purchase of land*) at the front of the sentence.

Nouns with compound adjectives

- A compound adjective consists of two words, usually with a hyphen between them. It generally comes before a noun.
- Compound adjectives are often used instead of relative clauses (▸ See **15** *Relative clauses*):

<u>Services that are run by the council</u> were suspended during the three-day public sector strike. → **Council-run services** were suspended during the three-day public sector strike.

The art gallery, <u>which had been newly restored,</u> was re-opened by the Mayor. → **The newly-restored art gallery** was re-opened by the Mayor.

The town's <u>music festival, which has received worldwide praise,</u> has run for 70 years. → The town's **internationally-acclaimed music festival** has run for 70 years.

Nouns with 'that ...' clauses

- A noun can be followed by a 'that ...' clause to form the subject of a verb:
  The proposition that a by-pass would solve the town's traffic problems was not accepted locally.
  Here, the bold part of the sentence forms the subject of the verb 'was not accepted'.

- A noun + 'that ...' clause can also come in the middle or at the end of a sentence:

  House prices fell when **the news that a by-pass might be built** was released.

  Local protest groups refused to accept **the view that the new road would reduce city centre traffic**.

- The following nouns are all commonly used with 'that ...' clauses:

idea, hypothesis, view, proposition	statement, news, warning	fact, rule, conclusion
likelihood, possibility, probability	assumption, belief, claim	danger, risk

Nouns describing feelings

- Instead of using the more common/informal adjectives to describe feelings, try to use nouns in these patterns.

  Officials were astonished when the scheme failed.

to the + noun + of	→	**To the astonishment of** officials, the scheme failed.
to + possessive + noun	→	**To their/officials' astonishment**, the scheme failed.
with + noun	→	Officials reacted **with astonishment** when the scheme failed.

> **! Danger Zone**
>
> **Omitting 'that'**
>
> In a **noun + 'that ...' clause**, the word *that* cannot be left out.
>
> The belief the situation was deteriorating was widespread among local residents. ✗
>
> **The belief that the situation was deteriorating** was widespread among local residents. ✓

Exercises

1 Complete the sentences with noun phrases.

1 The council have decided to construct a one-way system to reduce city-centre traffic.

  The .... a one-way system will allow the council to reduce city-centre traffic.

2 The chairperson questioned whether some of the research was relevant.

  The chairperson questioned the .... some of the research.

3 Local people were furious when they heard the announcement.

  Local people greeted the announcement ....

4 The town's provision of cheaper housing has been getting better in recent years.

  There have been .... the town's provision of cheaper housing in recent years.

5 The arena, which has been adapted specially, will host the athletics contest.

  The .... arena will host the athletics contest.

6 House prices have risen in the suburbs, which are expanding rapidly.

  House prices have risen in the .... suburbs.

2 Rewrite the sentences, replacing the underlined part with a noun phrase or compound adjective.

1 <u>Because it was likely that residents would object</u>, the proposal was withdrawn.

2 The council made final changes to the celebrations, <u>which had been carefully planned</u>.

3 Local councillors understood how <u>important</u> the theatre was to the town.

4 The view, <u>which many people held</u>, was that the council had acted too slowly.

3 Add the most appropriate missing word/phrase from this list to each sentence.

that/ the claim/ would resign/ was ignored/ might be found

1 The warning that the bridge was about to collapse by the council.

2 The editor was dismissive of that newspaper reports had exaggerated the costs of repairing the town hall.

3 The possibility that no funding for the museum was finally accepted by the curator and her colleagues.

4 There were complaints when the rule all councillors had to publish their expenses online was changed.

5 It was midnight before the statement that the Mayor was read out.

19   Commas 1 – correct uses

Commas are used to break up sentences so that they are clear and easy to follow.

> ### 💡 Writing Tip
>
> There are many occasions when a comma is optional, or when another form of punctuation, such as a dash or semi-colon could be used instead, but there are also many occasions when a comma is absolutely essential.

Commas separating clauses

▶ **Look carefully at the use of commas in these sentences from essays about international relations.**

Clauses with participles

Relations between the two countries became strained, **leading** to open hostility.
The talks **having broken down**, relations between the two countries became even more strained.
◗ See **34** *Participles*.

Non-defining relative clauses (giving additional information)

There was disagreement on a number of foreign policy issues, **which** caused relations between the two countries to become strained.

NOTE: You must not use a comma before a defining relative clause that gives essential information without which the sentence would not make sense:
These were among the issues which caused relations between the two countries to become strained.
◗ See **15** *Relative clauses*.

Clauses with linking words and phrases

Despite attempts to repair relations between the two countries**,** they deteriorated into open hostility.

NOTE: Before 'and', 'but' and 'because', you can use a comma or you can leave it out, but if the sentence is a long and complex one it is best to use a comma to make the sentence easier to read:
The talks broke down(,) and relations between the two countries deteriorated.
The talks were conducted against a background of increasing distrust between the representatives of both sides, and relations between the two countries deteriorated.

however, nevertheless, therefore, consequently, in addition, instead, as a result, on the other hand, furthermore, moreover
- Use a comma after these words if they begin a sentence:
  The talks were aimed at improving relations. **Instead**, they caused them to deteriorate.
- Use a comma before and after these words if they do not begin a sentence:
  The talks, **therefore**, did not achieve their aim of improving relations.
- If you use another linking word such as 'and' or 'but' before these words and phrases, it is not necessary to use a comma before that linking word:
  The talks broke down(,) **and as a result,** relations deteriorated even further.
  The talks broke down **and(,) as a result,** relations deteriorated even further.
  ◗ See **26, 27, 28** and **29** *Linking*.

Clauses within clauses

A sentence may have one clause inside another, rather than one complete clause after another. Use commas before and after a clause that comes within a clause:
Relations between the two countries, **which had not been cordial for some time**, deteriorated into open hostility.
The problem, **caused by a number of factors**, badly affected relations between them.

Sentences with more than two clauses

Separate each clause with a comma if one complete clause follows another:

Caused by a number of factors, the problem badly affected relations between them, which had previously been cordial.

- Put a comma before and after a clause within a clause and separate any other clauses with commas:

Relations between the two countries, **which had not been cordial for some time**, deteriorated into open hostility, **and** this lasted for over a decade.   ♦ See **2** *Parts of a sentence.*

Commas separating words and phrases

- Before a **quotation**:

The statement began, 'After many hours of talks, we have been unable to reach agreement.'

NOTE: You can also use a colon instead of a comma here.

♦ See **24** *Inverted commas.*

- With **references,** for example to give the name of someone or the title of something previously mentioned:

The Prime Minister at that time, Edward Heath, supported a peace formula in Northern Ireland.

The proposed agreement, the Sunningdale Agreement, was discussed at that meeting.

- When giving **extra, relevant information** about something or someone previously mentioned:

There was widespread rioting in the Falls Road, an area of Belfast.

- Separating **items in a list**:

The issues surrounding 'The Troubles' in Northern Ireland included sectarian violence, the idea of power-sharing, the province's relations with the rest of the United Kingdom(,) and terrorism on the mainland.

NOTE: A comma is not essential before the last item on the list, which begins with 'and'.

♦ See 'Punctuating lists' in **21** *Colons and semi-colons.*

- With **adverbs used instead of a clause**:

Attempts were made to find a solution. These attempts, unfortunately, were unsuccessful. / Unfortunately, these attempts were unsuccessful.

♦ See **50** *Adjectives and adverbs.*

- With these words and phrases: **of course, for example, namely:**

Of course, this incident led to retaliation.

There were numerous bombings in mainland Britain, for example in a pub in Birmingham.

A new organisation was formed, namely the Provisional IRA.

- **Before the year** in a date:

28th August, 2011

- **Before a town/city, state/county or country** if you are referring to a place in it:

Princeton, New Jersey

King's College, London

Helsinki, Finland.

- **Between adjectives** when more than one is used:

The Troubles in Northern Ireland were long, complex and painful.

NOTE: Use 'and' before the last adjective but not between any of the others.

> **Remember!**
> Read back every sentence you have written to make sure that you have put in commas where they are essential.

Exercise

Insert any necessary commas in this paragraph.

On July 20th 1969 having stepped onto the Moon's surface Neil Armstrong uttered the famous words 'One small step for man one giant leap for mankind.' Although it had been hoped that the moon landing would lead to significant advances in space travel some of which may soon become a reality the scientific progress has generally been slow. However space research has done much to unite nations. The establishment of the International Space Station the Space Shuttle and the Hubble Telescope illustrates how much easier and more profitable it is for nations to work as a team rather than in isolation.

20 Commas 2 – incorrect uses

Writing Tip

Even if the rest of your sentence is perfectly good, adding commas where they should not be used will automatically lower the standard of your work.

Remember!

Read back every sentence you have written to make sure that any commas you have put in really should be there.

Never use a comma

- **with a clause beginning 'that ...':**
  The exam results indicated, that children were improving at maths and science. ✗
  The Department of Education announced, that there would be reforms to the system. ✗

- **between a subject and its verb**
  Teachers with many years of experience, were beginning to leave the profession. ✗

- **between two subjects linked by 'and':**
  The professor, and his colleagues carried out important research into primary education in the UK. ✗

- **in a phrase involving a group of words that belong together as a single unit:**
  for example –

  between a noun or adjective and a preposition that goes with it:
  There was a considerable improvement, in the performance of boys in that age group. ✗
  Many in the teaching profession were enthusiastic, about the proposed changes to the curriculum. ✗

  between a verb and a word or phrase that goes with it:
  Parents in general viewed the changes, as a positive move. ✗
  Everyone was pleased because discipline in schooled continued, to improve each year. ✗
  Pupils were given the opportunity to vote, for members of their own council. ✗

  before 'or' if it comes between two adjectives, nouns or verbs:
  Pupils covered this subject in the second, or third year of their course. ✗
  Pupils could choose Spanish, or German as their second language. ✗
  Pupils were allowed to write, or type their answers. ✗

❗ Danger Zone

Comma 'splicing'

This term means incorrectly using a comma between what are in fact two complete sentences.

▶ **Look at this example of an incorrect sentence from an essay about graphic design.**

  Graphic design can be seen in many places in modern life, it extends well beyond the world of advertising. ✗

These are two separate sentences and cannot be separated by a comma. They could be correctly written:

- **using a linking word or phrase to form one correct sentence:**
  Graphic design can be seen in many places in modern life(,) and it extends well beyond the world of advertising. ✓

- **making two sentences with a full stop and a capital letter:**
  Graphic design can be seen in many places in modern life. It extends well beyond the world of advertising. ✓

- **linking the two sentences with a semi-colon (and no capital letter after it):**
  Graphic design can be seen in many places in modern life; it extends well beyond the world of advertising. ✓
  ↳ See **21** *Colons and semi-colons.*

Exercises

1 Decide whether these sentences are correct or not. Then make any necessary changes in the use of commas.

1 Professor Granger, and his team presented the results of their research, on the use of support staff in the classroom.

2 It used to be the case that children whose parents went to university were more likely to go on to higher education than those with parents who had gone straight into work.

3 Sociologists argue that streaming works in the favour of the top streams, where motivation levels amongst all parties are high.

4 In the lower streams on the other hand, there is little motivation amongst teachers to encourage students to do better with the inevitable result that they fail to progress.

5 The willingness of some children in the developing world to walk four or five miles to school each day stems from the very firm conviction that education opens the door of opportunity.

6 Course dates for some subjects have changed, you can find the changes on the relevant website.

7 Students can submit the application form, online or by mail.

2 Correct these sentences by adding commas, where appropriate.

1 As part of the course you will analyse the theoretical ideas of socialism conservatism and liberalism.

2 The Education Authority realising that primary and secondary schools in some areas had too many applicants devised a new admissions policy.

3 As the education plan proved to be flawed impractical and unprofitable it was quickly abandoned.

4 The Government has announced that students who live in rented accommodation may be eligible for financial assistance whatever their circumstances.

5 'Labelling' the act of saying that a child is of a certain type usually works to a child's disadvantage.

3 Insert commas in this paragraph, where they are appropriate.

According to this week's media in particular the mainstream newspapers class sizes in some British schools in the City of London are too big for Head Teachers to cope with and as a consequence some children are not fulfilling their academic potential. As a result of pressure from professionals in education the Mayor has ordered an official enquiry into the situation which will be run by Generating Genius a charitable organisation that has already helped some teenagers from poorer socio-economic backgrounds to get good university places. The enquiry, which will take place over the next ten months will look into a range of educational issues including overcrowding in classrooms improving overall standards and promoting relationships between state and independent schools. On 12th November the Mayor will speak at the Institute of Education Bedford where in the words of one reporter 'there will be considerable interest in what he has to say'. In the meantime in order to ensure that class sizes do not get out of hand it is possible that the Greater London Authority will take steps to alleviate the situation by for example allocating some of its own buildings to the education of its city's young people.

21 Colons & semi-colons

Colons

▶ **Read these sentences from a social studies essay and find the punctuation errors.**

A government report highlighted three main causes of crime in the inner city. High unemployment, poor housing and family breakdown. ✘

The report concluded as follows. 'Solving the problems of the inner city is not simply a question of providing money for initiatives.' ✘

The report raised one serious question, how could these problems best be addressed to improve quality of life for those in the inner city? ✘

The sentences should read:

	Rules
A government report highlighted three main causes of crime in the inner city: high unemployment, poor housing and family breakdown. ✔	← Colon before a list
The report concluded as follows: 'Solving the problems of the inner city is not simply a question of providing money for initiatives.' ✔	← Colon before a quotation
The report raised one serious question: how could these problems best be addressed to improve quality of life for those in the inner city? ✔	← Colon before an explanation of something just mentioned (what the 'serious question' is)

> **Remember!**
>
> Do not use a colon when reporting someone's words with 'that'.
>
> There are experts who say that: housing is the most important inner-city issue. ✘

Semi-colons

▶ **Now think about how semi-colons can be used in these sentences from the same social studies essay.**

A government report highlighted three main causes of crime in the inner city: there had been a considerable recent rise in unemployment and a significant number of people were living in poor housing conditions and family breakdown was a major factor in levels of youth crime. ✘

The report concluded that solving the problems of the inner city was not simply a question of providing money for initiatives – it also required a major change in attitudes. ✘

● Here are the sentences with semi-colons inserted. **These are the only ways that you can use semi-colons:**

	Rules
A government report highlighted three main causes of crime in the inner city: there had been a considerable recent rise in unemployment; a significant number of people were living in poor housing conditions; and family breakdown was a major factor in levels of youth crime. ✔	← Semi-colon between long phrases or sentences in a list. (Use 'and' with the last item in the list.)

The report concluded that solving the problems of the inner city was not simply a question of providing money for initiatives; it also required a major change in attitudes. ✓

← Semi-colon to separate two complete sentences where the second one continues a point made in the first

NOTE: In the second sentence (The report concluded…), the use of a dash or full-stop and capital letter are both also correct.

📋 Remember!

Do not use semi-colons where a comma is required.

Despite the construction of a ring-road; traffic congestion worsened. ✗

Despite the construction of a ring-road, traffic congestion worsened. ✓

❗ Danger Zone

Punctuating lists

Use colons and semi-colons to make lists of long phrases clear.

In the survey, people living in rural areas reported that their major concerns were as follows, lack of regular public transport services, the need to make car journeys to shop in retail parks, rising property prices due to homes being bought by wealthy outsiders and the loss of jobs in agricultural and related industries. ✗

To be readable, this list needs a colon and some semi-colons:

In the survey, people living in rural areas reported that their major concerns were as follows: lack of regular public transport services; the need to make car journeys to shop in retail parks; rising property prices due to homes being bought by wealthy outsiders; and the loss of jobs in agricultural and related industries. ✓

The colon introduces the list and the semi-colons separate the items in the list.

"Don't forget about us!"

Exercises

1 Insert colons and/or semi-colons in the sentences.

1 The report focuses on three issues how reliable public transport systems are what measures would be most effective in reducing traffic congestion and whether parking facilities are adequate.
2 Most reports on the inner city focus on problems in fact there have been many improvements too.
3 This leads us to another very important development in town planning the arrival of out-of-town shopping centres.
4 Tomlinson was correct when he made the statement 'Urban planners should always aim to avoid demolishing historic buildings.'
5 Among town planners today, there is one buzzword sustainability.

2 One of these sentences is correct. Find the punctuation mistakes in the other four sentences and correct them.

1 This brings me to my final point; the repercussions of local government initiatives have not always been carefully considered.
2 The problem was not confined to one area; it was widespread throughout the country.
3 The drive to create a sustainable environment raises a serious question, to what extent should function take precedence over form?
4 People who argue that: cities are becoming overcrowded should ask themselves why.
5 In some societies, homes need to be built to accommodate a range of family structures that include extended families; nuclear families; and single-parent households.

22 Hyphens, dashes & brackets

A **hyphen** (-) has no space before or after it: *semi-detached*.
A **dash** (–) has a space both before and after it: *It worked – but only for a short time.*
Brackets () must come in pairs: (*in other words, one at the beginning and one at the end*).

> **Writing Tip**
>
> Hyphens are not used these days as much as they used to be, but there are certain times when you should use a hyphen. Brackets and dashes can be used effectively in academic work to separate information in sentences.

Hyphens

You should use a hyphen:

- between parts of an **adjective** formed from **two or more complete words**:

  middle-aged user-friendly customer-driven

- after certain prefixes: e.g. **semi, ex, counter, e, self**

  semi-detached ex-colleague counter-productive
  e-commerce self-conscious

  with **co** if referring to people: co-author co-founder

> **Remember!**
>
> Hyphens are not generally used after most prefixes, e.g. underestimate, multinational.
>
> It is not a major mistake to use a hyphen after a prefix when one is not normally used, but it is better only to use them in the ways listed here.

- for words consisting of **a number and another word**: a three-stage process
- for an **age** used as an adjective: a 40-year-old man BUT *40 years old*
- in phrases beginning **well** and with certain other phrases, only if they are used **before a noun**:

  state-of-the-art equipment up-to-date information well-planned courses long-term solutions

  BUT – *The equipment is state of the art. / keep up to date with all the latest information*
  a club that is well known for its friendliness / a plan that might work in the long term

You can use a hyphen:

- when writing **numbers** between 21 and 99 and fractions in words: seventy-five, two-thirds
- for **surnames** consisting of two different names: the inventor of the worldwide web, Tim Berners-Lee

Dashes

You can use dashes:

- at the end of a sentence to **add a thought or comment** on what has just been said:
  Strict dietary guidelines for the playing squad transformed their fitness levels – to an astonishing degree.
  NOTE: Don't overuse dashes. This might make your work too informal in style.
- at the end of a sentence to **summarise or conclude** what has gone before:
  Team morale, performance in matches and the response of fans were all transformed by this new mental approach among the players – in short, it improved everything.
  NOTE: You could use a semi-colon instead of the dash here.

Brackets

You should use brackets:

- for **cross-references**: This is also important with regard to fitness conditioning (see also Section 3).
- for **sources of information**, such as authors, researchers, books, reports, etc., particularly if you are quoting from them, and for **years**:
  One study found that fitness was 'not the major factor in successful performance' (Gregory, 2004).
- around **numbers or letters** for separate points in a sentence:
  They won, not because they were the better team but because (a) they had prepared better than their opponents and (b) they were more focused during the game.
  NOTE: You should not do this for more than two or at most three points. For a longer list, use semi-colons.

You can use brackets:

- at the **end** of a sentence to **add information that is not essential**:

  Results improved a great deal (though there were occasional defeats).

- for a **whole sentence** that adds **extra but not essential** information:

  All of these studies indicated that diet and lifestyle were as important as skill and fitness with regard to differences in results for the very top players. (This was not the case for average players but our focus here is on top players.)

  NOTE: The full stop that ends the full sentence must come before the second bracket.

Dashes or brackets

You can use dashes or brackets:

- in the **middle** of a sentence to **add information that is not essential** but may be useful or interesting, without interrupting the flow of the sentence:

  Strict dietary guidelines for members of the playing squad – a relatively recent innovation at that time – transformed their levels of fitness.

  Strict dietary guidelines for members of the playing squad (a relatively recent innovation at that time) transformed their levels of fitness.

  NOTE: Commas could also be used here instead of dashes or brackets.

- to **explain** something that has just been mentioned in a sentence:

  The practice of visualising – imagining yourself at key points during a game – proved to be very helpful.

  The practice of visualising (imagining yourself at key points during a game) proved to be very helpful.

Exercises

1 Add hyphens where they are required.

1 This was a well received reform at the time. Prior to it, only upper class people had been able to vote.
2 The records were not up to date and an old fashioned system was still in place.
3 His codefendant in the case was his former boss, and after a three month trial, they were both found guilty.
4 By the time he was thirty years old, he had a high powered job advising the government on state run services.
5 Countries wanted self determination and the status of being fully independent.

2 Use dashes where they are appropriate.

1 Opponents questioned the logic of his argument much to his annoyance.
2 He made a speech in the House of Commons and this was not the only time when he went against his own party in which he heavily criticised the policy.
3 Mistakes were made, inefficiency dogged the entire project, and complaints came in from all sides, this was not how things were supposed to be.
4 Pensioners regardless of their personal and financial circumstances were all better off because of this change.

3 Use brackets where they are appropriate.

1 There were exceptions to this pattern but the results were generally very consistent. Exceptions are listed in the table below. It was therefore possible to draw firm conclusions.
2 He was a strong supporter of entry into the eurozone and played a significant role in the country's decision to take that step. He later regretted this but that was far in the future.
3 In her influential report Approaches to Poverty 2005, Browne proposed wholesale changes to welfare rules.
4 The unforeseen consequence fewer workers having job security seriously affected morale in the industry.

23   Apostrophes

▶ **Read these sentences on the subject of US history and find the punctuation errors.**

There can be no doubt that Kennedys assassination marked a turning point and that it contributed to the upheaval that took place in the 1960's in the US. ✖

The Vietnam War and it's repercussions had a profound influence on US society and its a subject that still arouses strong feelings. ✖

What's wrong: There is one missing apostrophe and one apostrophe that should not be there in each sentence. The sentences should read:

There can be no doubt that **Kennedy's** assassination marked a turning point and that it contributed to the upheaval that took place in the **1960s** in the US. ✔

The Vietnam War and **its** repercussions had a profound influence on US society and **it's** a subject that still arouses strong feelings. ✔

Nouns & names

Use an apostrophe and s ('s) when something belongs to, is connected with or is done by someone or something:

- after a name
  <u>Barack Obama's</u> presidency/party/policies
- after a singular noun
  the <u>government's</u> policies/popularity/mistakes
- after a name or singular noun ending with **s**
  <u>Keynes's</u> economic theories/ his boss's actions
  NOTE: Instead of using a word ending **s's**, you can create a different phrase:
  Mauritius's population → *The population of Mauritius*
- after a plural noun that does not end with 's'
  <u>people's</u> opinions

Use an apostrophe (but not s):

- after plural nouns that end with s
  <u>politicians'</u> reactions / girls' and boys' ideas

Numbers

Do not use an apostrophe:

- with decades
  the 1980s
- with any other number (e.g. age)
  when he was in his 40s / forties
- for plurals (e.g. products)
  Levi 501s

Capital letters

Do not use an apostrophe:

- for plurals
  CDs for sale

Use an apostrophe and s ('s):

- with the meaning belonging to, connected with or done by, including when an organisation ends with **s**
  The CIA's activities/the IRS's tax rules

Contracted verbs

Use an apostrophe:

- when part of a verb is missing because it has been abbreviated:

the country's changing	→	the country is changing
it's changing	→	it is changing
they've decided	→	they have decided
you'll discover	→	you will discover
who's right?	→	who is right?
they couldn't respond	→	they could not respond

! Danger Zone

- **it's / its**

  it's = it is / it has
  its taken a long time ✗
  it's taken a long time ✓

  its = belonging to or connected with it
  in all of it's history ✗
  in all of **its history** ✓

- **they're / their**

  they're = they are
  their = belonging to or connected with them

  The speakers were popular because they're ideas resonated with the public. ✗
  The speakers were popular because **their ideas** resonated with the public. ✓

- **who's / whose**

  who's = who is/ who has
  whose is used before a noun with a possessive meaning

  Ghandi was a politician who's influence on the world was enormous. ✗
  Ghandi was a politician **whose influence** on the world was enormous. ✓

- **hers / ours/ yours / theirs**
  Do not use an apostrophe with these possessive words:

  Having won the election, the future was all their's. ✗
  Having won the election, the future was all **theirs**. ✓

Exercises

1 Insert apostrophes in the correct places in the following sentences.

1 The beneficial effect of Vitamin D on childrens health has been noted in recent research findings.
2 Apparently Ferraris latest supercar can reach speeds of over 200 miles per hour.
3 The development of teenagers identities is heavily influenced by their peers behaviour.
4 People have enjoyed Beethovens music for more than two hundred years.
5 Ive always believed that a designers most successful approach is to follow his intuition, rather than pander to clients ideas.

2 Correct the following sentences by inserting or removing apostrophes where necessary. You may also need to change the form of some words.

1 Sales of DVDs rose rapidly during the period, and they're ascendancy over video's was soon confirmed.
2 Cinema-going reached its height in the 1940's, when its escapist appeal attracted audiences wanting to see movie stars who's lives seemed incredibly glamorous.
3 In some experts views, the EUs target of 10 per cent biofuel use by 2020 is over-ambitious.
4 Boeing 747s are among the most commonly used commercial aircraft, and many million's of travellers have used them.
5 Research into people in their 20's indicates that their's is the first generation to be confronted by this problem, and many of them cant find a way to deal with it.

24 Inverted commas

Inverted commas can be single (') or double ("). When used for quoting actual words used by people in speech or written material, they are also called 'quotation marks' or 'speech marks'.

▶ **Read this paragraph from a social studies essay and notice how inverted commas are used, and how other punctuation is used with them:**

This report was considered 'ground-breaking' at the time because it indicated that changes in attitudes at all levels of society were taking place. 'The established patterns of family life are being broken,' the report stated, 'and this is having a major impact on the lives of a great many people.' The report began by looking at what these 'established patterns' were and went on to detail the 'drastic changes' that were taking place. It concluded: 'Whether or not people in general are happy about it, the truth is that society is changing forever.'

Quoting

- use a **colon** after a word meaning **said**:
  In their report, the researchers stated: 'Our findings will have far-reaching consequences on policy-makers.'
  NOTE: Notice the use of a capital letter at the beginning of the quotation and a full stop at the end of it, both inside the inverted commas because the quotation is a full sentence.

- use **two sets of inverted commas** if you put the speaker/writer **in the middle of a quotation**:
  'Our findings will have far-reaching consequences on the policy-makers,' the researchers stated in their report, 'as they suggest that current thinking is based on false assumptions.'
  NOTE: Notice the position of commas – before the second inverted comma for the first part of the quotation, and before the first inverted comma for the second part of the quotation.

- use three **dots** to indicate that some of the quotation has been left out:
  'Our findings … suggest that current thinking is based on false assumptions.'
  'Our findings […] suggest that current thinking is based on false assumptions.'
  NOTE: When you do this the resulting quotation must make complete sense.

- put inverted commas at the beginning and end of a **quoted phrase**, to make clear that it is a quotation and **not your own words**:
  The researchers pointed to the 'far-reaching consequences' of their findings.

- use a question mark or exclamation mark **before the second inverted comma** if it is part of the quotation:
  'What would the consequences of their findings be for policy-makers?' the researchers asked.
  NOTE: There is no comma after the second inverted comma if a question mark or exclamation mark is used.

- use a full stop **after the second inverted comma** if the quotation is not a whole sentence.
  The researchers said that current thinking was 'based on false assumptions'.

- use a **comma** and then the second inverted comma if the sentence does not end with the quotation:
  'Our findings will have far-reaching consequences on policy-makers,' the researchers stated in their report.

Remember!

Do not use inverted commas when you are paraphrasing someone's words rather than quoting the exact words.

The researchers claimed that 'their report would have far-reaching consequences'. ✗
The researchers claimed that their report would have far-reaching consequences. ✓

▶ See **46** *Paraphrasing*.

Other uses of inverted commas

- for a **term** that **may not be generally known, used or understood**

  The researchers used an 'extremes filtering' method to collate the results of their survey. This involved removing people with the highest and lowest scores from their calculations.

- for the **title** of a book, report, magazine, film, painting, etc.

  The researchers published their report, 'Changing Demographics: A Guide for Policy Makers' in the journal 'Social Indicators'.

  NOTE: Both titles could be in italics, without inverted commas.

- to indicate that you believe that something **is not or may not be true**

  This kind of research is regarded as 'challenging the status quo' but it often has no impact on policy-makers.

- to **highlight a word or phrase to be focused on**, which has already been mentioned in the piece

  They make much of the potential impact of their report. But what exactly is this 'impact' likely to be?

ⓘ Danger Zone

Inverted commas within inverted commas

Sometimes you need to use one set of inverted commas inside another, for example when a quotation includes something else that needs to be inside inverted commas.

If you are using single inverted commas throughout your work, use double inverted commas for the quotation within, and vice versa:

The researchers stated: 'We regard many current assumptions, especially those regarding what are commonly called "disadvantaged people", as both faulty and unhelpful.'

The researchers stated: "We regard many current assumptions, especially those regarding what are commonly called 'disadvantaged people', as both faulty and unhelpful."

There are no strict rules about whether you should use single or double, but you must use one or the other consistently.

Exercises

1 Decide if these sentences are correctly punctuated or not, and correct those which are not.

1 'There are many different ways of accessing the information' the manual stated.

2 In a letter to his family, he wrote: 'I am beginning to think that perhaps the artistic life is not for me'.

3 He was once quoted as saying that he 'would never consider making a return to politics'.

4 'Why do certain people have these behaviour patterns?', she asks at the beginning of her paper.

5 'The case for equal rights for all minorities,' she said in the speech, 'cannot be opposed in any real democracy.'

6 One expert stated that the situation 'would not improve significantly ...' '... for a considerable period of time.'

2 Add inverted commas where they are necessary or appropriate.

1 In his paper The Impact of the Internet, he argued that too little attention was being paid to what he called the sudden intrusion. By this he meant the speed at which the internet took over people's lives. These days, he said, people have lost the ability to think for themselves and to use their own initiative.

2 Organisations often describe themselves in their own literature as being open and accountable. One company I looked at in this research used the term open accountability when discussing this issue. But what do companies mean by this?

3 After the first day of conference, the leaders announced in their official statement We feel that we have made significant progress towards a solution on this difficult question. They also spoke of the extremely cordial relations we enjoy. We anticipate a further announcement after tomorrow's negotiations, they added.

25   Capital letters

Use capital letters for:

People

- the **name of a person**: Martin Simpson
- **a person's title**, e.g. Mr, Mrs, Ms, Professor, President, Prime Minister, Sir, etc.: Professor Olivia Peters / President Nixon / Prime Minister

Places

- a **building** or **landmark**: Westminster Abbey / Sydney Opera House
- a **geographical feature**: the (River) Thames / Mount Everest / Yosemite National Park / the Himalayas
- a **street** or **district**: Hollywood Boulevard / the district of Kensington in London
- the name of a **village/town/city, county, state** or **region**: Los Angeles / California / Scandinavia
- a **country** or **continent**: the capital city of Wales / in Africa / the United Arab Emirates
  NOTE: With **north, south, eastern, western,** etc. only use a capital if it is part of the name of a country or region: South Africa / South-East Asia / in the southern states of America

Days and months (but not seasons)

November / Saturday / in the winter

Planets

the Earth / Jupiter / Mars / the Moon

Nationalities and languages

French politicians / speak French / the Spanish

Historical periods and events

the Middle Ages / the Russian Revolution

Titles of published/media works

- **books**: War and Peace / Lord of the Rings
- **films, TV programmes**: Titanic / Gone with the Wind / News at Ten / Who Wants to be a Millionaire?
- **magazines, newspapers, journals**: the Daily Telegraph / the South China Morning Post / The Economist / the journal Nature
- **articles** and **academic papers**: in her article 'How Life has Changed for the Middle Classes'

NOTE: Small words such as 'a', 'the', 'and' or prepositions are not usually in capital letters for these titles, unless they are the first word of the title.
These titles could all be put in italics or inverted commas.

Job titles

the Head Teacher / the company's Chief Accountant / she has become Assistant Manager
NOTE: Do not use capital letters for a type of job, only use them for the actual job title: She is a senior manager at the company. / She is the company's Senior Production Manager.

Places of study and courses

- the name of a university, college, school: She is studying at the University of Sussex. / He is a student at Sydney University. / She went to Langland Comprehensive School.
  NOTE: Use 'the' only if the word University, College, School, etc. is the first word of the institution's name: the University of Toronto **NOT** the Warwick University
  NOTE: Do not a use a capital if you do not name the place: go to university / at school
- **departments**: the English Faculty / the Drama Department
  NOTE: Use 'the' before department names.
- **course titles**: She has a degree in Applied Mathematics.
  NOTE: Don't use capitals when talking generally about a subject area: A knowledge of statistics is vital for students.
- **examinations and qualifications**: International Baccalaureate / A Level / Bachelor of Arts

Organisations, official bodies and political parties, laws, treaties

Amnesty International / the International Criminal Court / the Red Crescent / the Labour Party / Greenpeace / the European Union / the Geneva Convention / the Human Rights Act / the Maastricht Treaty

Government institutions

Parliament / the House of Representatives / Congress / the Civil Service / the Department of Transport

Companies

Lloyd's Bank / Starbucks / Amazon / News International

NOTE: 'Ltd' and 'plc' are usually used with full company names: Harston & Sons Ltd / Uniframe plc

Brand names

Sony Walkman / Ford Mondeo

Abbreviations

Use capitals for **all** letters of abbreviations:

the BBC / the UN / UNESCO / NSPCC
in the UK / the US government
an MP / the CEO / the HR Department
CV / CRB form
DVD / CD / PC
BSc / MBA

NOTE: The plural of any abbreviation has no apostrophe: MPs voted to ... / the sales of DVDs

An apostrophe is only used for a possessive: an MP's salary / that CD's sales ...   ▶ See **23** *Apostrophes*.

 Remember!

- Use a capital letter to begin a sentence (and a full stop to end it).
  There are several reasons for this unusual turn of events.
- Use capital letters to address the person you are writing to in a letter or email.
  Dear Mr Davies,

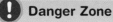 **Danger Zone**

Misusing capital letters

- Do not use capital letters for ordinary nouns that cannot be regarded as names.
  This is a problem that affects Society in a great many ways. ✗
  This is a problem that affects society in a great many ways. ✓
- Do not use capital letters to emphasise a point, as you might in informal writing such as an email to a friend:
  This was an EXTREMELY IMPORTANT matter that had to be dealt with urgently. ✗
  This was an extremely important matter that had to be dealt with urgently. ✓

Exercise

Correct the following sentences by changing letters to capitals, where necessary.

1 The amazon rainforest is two-thirds the size of the us, yet home to more than 30 million people and one in ten of the earth's species.

2 Due to the screening of the mexican grand prix, this week's quiz show, 'send me a line', will be broadcast on itv at the earlier time of 5.00 pm on friday.

3 Farmers in the ivory coast barely make a living, while the cocoa produced there feeds the world's chocolate industry.

4 The folk artist, steve knightly, mixes music and legend on his latest cd, 'cruel river'.

5 In his book, the end of poverty, Jeffrey d. sachs looks at how some of the world's poorest people can improve their standard of living.

6 To go to university in north america, it is better to take the international baccalaureate than A levels.

7 The flood seriously affected homes in the north-west of England and completely destroyed the 100-year-old premises of grandacre and sons in preston.

8 Last week, the uk border agency announced that it would be making a number of changes in line with government policy.

9 The renaissance was a period just before the modern era when great developments took place across europe in art and literature.

10 In her paper, 'talking in twos', Amanda Pritchard examines a new approach to raising bilingual children.

26   Linking: contrasting

A **linker** connects sentences or parts of sentences. Linkers may be words → but, however, etc.

or phrases → in spite of, on the other hand.

 Writing Tip

Sophisticated linking allows you to present contrasting ideas more clearly, and makes it easier for the reader to absorb information.

▶ **Read this introductory paragraph to an essay about the Welfare State in Britain and look at how the ideas and points are connected.**

The Welfare State in Britain was created immediately after the Second World War but British society has changed a great deal since then. Aspects of the Welfare State, such as the NHS and the old-age pension, have been regarded as untouchable by every political party, but some experts say this should not continue to be the case. It is desirable to have a 'safety net' for the poorest in society, they say, but it is not economically sustainable for the taxpayer to fund all these benefits.

What's wrong: The linking of points and ideas is too basic and repetitive; everything is linked with 'but'. More varied and sophisticated linking words and phrases could be used to give the paragraph a more academic style and to make the points clearer.

● Here is the paragraph with better linking:

The Welfare State in Britain was created immediately after the Second World War. **However**, British society has changed a great deal since then. **Although** aspects of the Welfare State, such as the NHS and the old-age pension, have been regarded as untouchable by every political party, some experts say this should not continue to be the case. **While** it is desirable to have a 'safety net' for the poorest in society, they say, it is not economically sustainable for the taxpayer to fund all these benefits.

● Here are some examples of how contrastive linkers are used:

although/while/whereas
● At the beginning of or between the clauses of a single sentence; commas separate clauses:
  Although/while/whereas some historians regard it as a great success, others point to faults.

  OR

  Some historians regard it as a great success, **although/while/whereas** others point to faults.

even though
● For greater emphasis than 'although':
  Even though it is a key part of British society, the Welfare State has its critics.

whilst
● More formal than 'while':
  Whilst it is a key part of British society, the Welfare State has its critics.

> **Remember!**
>
> Many words can be used instead of 'but' to link contrasting or contradictory points or pieces of information.

'However'

However must be used in these ways.

1 At the beginning of a new sentence, followed by a comma.
   Some historians regard the Welfare State as a great success. **However**, others point to faults. ✔
   'However' cannot be used to join two parts of a single sentence.
   Some historians regard it as a great success however others point to faults. ✘

2 Within a second sentence, surrounded by commas.
   Some historians regard the Welfare State as a great success. Others, **however**, point to faults. ✔
   'However' cannot be used without commas.
   Some historians regard it as a great success. Others however point to faults. ✘

nevertheless

● At the beginning of a new sentence followed by a comma or in a second sentence, surrounded by commas:
   The Welfare State is a key part of British society. **Nevertheless**, it has its critics.
   The Welfare State is a key part of British society. People point out, **nevertheless**, that it does have many critics.

despite/in spite of

● Followed by 'the fact that', a noun or '-ing'; comma separates parts of the sentence:
   Despite the fact that it is a key part of British society, the Welfare State has its critics.
   Despite its position as a key part of British society, the Welfare State has its critics.
   In spite of being a key part of British society, the Welfare State has its critics.

Exercises

1 Use the word in brackets to improve the linking in the sentences.

1 The number of annual visitors to the Galapagos Islands is around 170,000 but in 1991 it was 41,000. (*whilst*)
2 Economic predictions are optimistic but business confidence has fallen over the past few months. (*despite*)
3 Weather data has been collected in Britain for 350 years but opinions differ on how reliable that data is. (*however*)
4 A dispersant was sprayed onto the oil slick but thousands of seabirds were washed up along the beach. (*even though*)
5 Some businesses invest heavily in researching new products but others prefer to allocate more funds to marketing. (*whereas*)

2 Correct the following. Do not change the linking word or phrase used.

1 It is a well-known fact that conservation projects can be costly nevertheless they need to be prioritised.
2 Although some parents believe in the benefits of home tutoring. Most think that children require the school environment for the full development of their social skills.
3 In spite of the medical profession give warnings people still smoke.
4 Social networking sites were designed to develop new friendships however their main use has been to communicate with existing peer groups.
5 Whilst most film festivals in the world show one or two German movies but films 'Made in Germany' are not given the recognition they deserve.

27 Linking: adding

1st part of linking phrase   2nd part of linking phrase

Not only were the existing facilities sub-standard, **but they were also** expensive to maintain.

> 💡 **Writing Tip**
>
> Using linking words and phrases that are not as simple as the ones you might use in conversation can enable you to connect and emphasise ideas and facts in a coherent, effective way.

▶ **Read this paragraph from a business case study on a company and look at how the points are connected.**

Sealtrack modernised their factory in Thirsk and they invited management consultants TPS to conduct an audit of their staff development provision and make recommendations. Very few Sealtrack staff had applied for funds to upgrade their qualifications, according to TPS, and the internal workshops had little relevance to the actual needs of participants and were poorly attended.

What's wrong: The over-use of 'and' to link the ideas makes the linking too simplistic.

● Here is the paragraph with better linking:

In addition to modernising their factory in Thirsk, Sealtrack invited management consultants TPS to conduct an audit of their staff-development provision and make recommendations. **Not only** had very few Sealtrack staff applied for funds to upgrade their qualifications, according to TPS, **but also** the internal workshops had little relevance to the actual needs of participants, and were poorly attended.

● Here are some examples of how linkers for adding information are used:

also/as well
● **also** is often used between a subject and a verb:
Although this essay will focus mainly on UK companies, it will **also** consider one or two French businesses.
● **as well** is often used at the end of a sentence:
Although this essay will focus mainly on UK companies, it will consider one or two French businesses **as well**.

in addition to/as well as/besides
● at the beginning or in the middle of a sentence
1 + -ing
In addition to/As well as/Besides buying up smaller companies, Welltech are making exclusive deals with supermarket chains.
Welltech are making exclusive deals with supermarket chains **in addition to/as well as/besides buying** up smaller companies.

2 + noun
In addition to/As well as/Besides its factories in France, Welltech has a series of retail outlets in Switzerland under the name 'Mangebien'.

> 📋 **Remember!**
>
> **Besides** meaning *in addition to* is different from *beside* meaning *near/next to* (e.g. *beside the sea.*) Don't confuse the two!

moreover/furthermore/in addition
● to emphasise the information that follows
● at the beginning of a sentence followed by a comma, or later, surrounded by commas
Sealtrack has improved its in-house staff development programme. **In addition**, more than 30 per cent of its workforce are now taking part-time courses at local colleges.
Sealtrack has improved its in-house staff development programme. More than 30 per cent of its workforce, **furthermore**, are now taking part-time courses at local colleges.

not only ... but also
Welltech is **not only** a manufacturer **but also** a successful retailer of food products.

● when **not only** is placed at the beginning for greater emphasis, you need to use the same pattern as for questions: **not only + auxiliary + subject + verb**

Not only **is Welltech** a manufacturer but it is also a successful retailer of food products.
Not only **did Welltech expand** its operation in Europe, but it also formed a partnership in America.

> **❗ Danger Zone**
> **Punctuation**
>
> It is a mistake to use linkers such as 'furthermore', 'moreover', 'in addition' in the middle of a single sentence, without punctuation:
> Sealtrack has improved its in-house staff development programme moreover more than 30 per cent of its workforce is now taking part-time courses at local colleges. ❌
> Sealtrack has improved its in-house staff development programme; **moreover**, more than 30 per cent of its workforce is now taking part-time courses at local colleges. ✔
>
> A comma is required at the end of the clause if a sentence begins with 'in addition to', 'as well as', 'besides':
> **In addition to** addressing staff needs, development sessions should focus on company objectives. ✔

with
● to give details about what is stated in the other part of the sentence
● used instead of an 'and' clause

  1 + noun
  The company had a very successful year, **with profits** of £3.2m. (= and it had/made/reported profits of ....)

  2 + noun + -ing
  The company had a very successful year, **with profits rising** from £1.7m to £3.3m. (= and profits rose from ...)

Exercises

1 Correct the following. Do not change the linking word or phrase used.

  1 Raw materials are becoming more expensive, in addition the fuel costs involved in transporting them are increasing.
  2 Beside improving staff performance, staff development opportunities tend to increase employees' loyalty to the company.
  3 Not only Sealtrack is winning contracts in the private sector, it is also bidding successfully for major projects in the public sector.
  4 A new recruitment process was introduced, with its impressive results.
  5 Changing the layout of the factory would be very expensive. It could furthermore delay production for several months.
  6 Having so far done most of their business in the UK, Sealtrack is now as well developing products for the American market.

2 Rewrite the sentences, following the instructions in brackets.

  1 Fast Track Solutions was declared bankrupt and its CEO was given a six-year prison sentence for fraud. (Start with *Not only ... .*)
  2 Welltech made record profits in 2011 and it won an award for its staff development programme. (Start with *As well as ... .*)
  3 Sealtrack's braking system is the most technologically advanced on the market. It is selling at the cheapest price at the moment as well. (Use *moreover* instead of *as well.*)
  4 Compro streamlined its management structure and 52 middle managers were made redundant. (Use *with* in the middle of the sentence.)
  5 Grigson plc have increased their market share in the UK and won new contracts in Spain. (Use *in addition to* in the middle of the sentence.)
  6 Welltech lowered production costs at its factory and improved quality. (Start with *Not only ... .*)

28　Linking: causes

Result　　　　　　linker　　+　　cause

There have been fewer accidents, **owing to** improved health and safety measures.

 Writing Tip

In conversation, causes and results are often described using simple words like 'and', 'because' and 'so'. In academic writing, the inclusion of some more sophisticated words and phrases will create a good impression.

▶ **Read this paragraph from a sociology essay and look at how the causes and results are connected.**

The closure of a series of coal mines in the UK during the 1980s **brought about** a severe rise in regional unemployment. **Since** many of the pit towns and villages had relied almost entirely on the local mine as a source of work, very few alternatives were available to local men of employable age. **Due to the fact that** employment prospects were so bleak, many of them came to the conclusion that their working lives were effectively finished.

Verbs

cause/bring about
1 + noun
The Industrial Revolution **caused/brought about the growth** of the city.
The growth of cities in Britain was **caused/brought about by** the Industrial revolution.

2 + object + infinitive
The Industrial Revolution **caused people to leave** their villages for the city.

trigger + noun
● = 'cause to happen'; used for describing a dramatic or sudden event or development
The Industrial Revolution **triggered** wholesale changes in the way of life of working people.

Linkers connecting parts of a sentence

because/because of
1 because + subject + verb
The slimming drug was withdrawn **because it had** serious long-term side-effects.

2 because of + noun
The slimming drug was withdrawn **because of serious long-term side-effects**.

as/since
● more formal than 'because'
● often used at the beginning of a sentence to introduce a cause
As/Since the slimming drug had serious long-term side effects, it was withdrawn.

due to/owing to/on account of
● formal and appropriate in academic writing
1 + noun
Due to/Owing to/On account of adverse publicity about its side effects, the slimming drug was withdrawn.

2 + the fact that + subject, verb, etc.
Due to/Owing to/On account of the fact that it received adverse publicity about its side effects, the slimming drug was withdrawn.

3 + noun + -ing
Due to the slimming drug receiving adverse publicity about its side effects, it was withdrawn.

Grammatical use of due to/owing to/on account of

'Due to'/'owing to'/'On account of' are not followed by a subject, verb, etc.

Due to people were consuming so much junk food, instances of dangerous obesity increased. ✗

You have to use one of the grammatical structures listed above:

On account of the high consumption of junk food, ... ✓
Owing to the fact that people were consuming so much junk food, ... ✓
Due to people consuming so much junk food, ... ✓

on the grounds that ...

● = because; often used for the reason given by someone (= the cause)
  + subject, verb, etc.
  Experts called for an increase in the prices of alcoholic drinks in supermarkets **on the grounds that** this would reduce alcohol consumption.
  On the grounds that it would reduce alcohol consumption, experts called for an increase in the prices of alcoholic drinks in supermarkets

Remember!

Instead of using 'because' and 'because of' all the time, use some of the above words and phrases.

which + be/explain + why

Many people work long hours, **which is/explains why** they often consume convenience foods.

Nouns

cause (of) / source (of) + noun

The cause of hypothermia is normally an overexposure to extremely cold temperatures.
One source of high blood pressure may be an excessive intake of salt in the sufferer's diet.

reason for + noun / reason why + subject, verb, etc.

The main **reason for the improvement** in the patients' cardiovascular and pulmonary functions was the course of aerobic exercise that they had undertaken.
The main **reason why the patients' cardiovascular and pulmonary functions improved** was the course of aerobic exercise that they had undertaken.

Exercises

1 Correct the sentences.

1 Crime rates have risen in this part of the city, and is why so many residents have sold up and left.
2 On account the fact that the museum and gallery were able to attract private sector sponsorship, their short-term future seems secure.
3 The increased power of the media to question and criticise may have brought a lack of respect for politicians.
4 The research facility was closed because serious concerns about its standards of health and safety.
5 One reason of an episode of hyperactivity in children may be the excessive consumption of sugar.
6 A number of basic errors were made due to no trained medical staff were present at the time.

2 Rewrite the sentences, using the words in brackets.

1 Many citizens are dissatisfied with the way in which lobbyists influence Government policy. This means that there are often calls for reform. (*Since*)
2 The public is concerned because of the possible use of genetic testing by insurance companies. (*one source of*)
3 Some adolescents appear to suffer from headaches and anxiety because of their repeated poor performance in computer games. (*due*)
4 Because they would affect their trade, local shopkeepers attacked the new parking charges. (*grounds*)
5 Syms argues that an apparently trivial event may cause a period of mental illness. (*triggered*)

29 Linking: results

cause   linker   +   result

There were too many layers of management. **As a result**, efficiency decreased.

Writing Tip

Try to vary the way you link results and their causes and to clarify their relative importance. Sometimes it is necessary to emphasise the result, rather than the cause, as in the example above.

▶ **Read this paragraph from an essay on stress in the workplace and look at how results and their causes are connected:**

Burnout in the workplace can happen **as a result of** prolonged stress. Initial symptoms may **stem from** the desire of an employee to do well and to fit into the corporate structure. An unrealistic deadline from a senior manager can then **lead to** additional pressure on the individual, which may become **so severe that** he or she is unable to continue functioning in the workplace.

Verbs

result from/stem from

1 + noun
- followed by the cause of something:
  An inability to think clearly at work may simply **result/stem from** a lack of sleep.

2 + object + -ing
Stress at work can **result from employees feeling** that they are badly treated by management.

lead to /result in /produce
- followed by the result:

  1 + noun
  Changes in management and systems **led to/resulted in/produced** problems for many of the staff.

  2 + object + -ing
  Changes in management and systems **led to/resulted in some employees leaving** the company.

  3 the present participle (-ing form)
  There were constant changes of management personnel, **resulting in/producing** confusion among the workforce.

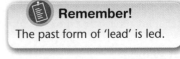

Remember!
The past form of 'lead' is led.

Linkers connecting clauses and sentences

so /such .... that ...
- used for linking a cause with its result in these patterns:

  1 so + adjective/adverb + that
  Change was **so rapid that** many employees struggled to keep pace with it.
  Change was introduced **so rapidly that** many employees struggled to keep pace with it.

  2 such + noun + that
  There was **such rapid change that** many employees struggled to keep pace with it.

as a result
- at the beginning of a second sentence, followed by a comma:
  The company culture became more authoritarian and less caring. **As a result**, morale among staff fell.
- mid-sentence, after 'and' with commas before and after:
  The company culture became more authoritarian and, **as a result**, morale among staff fell.

- also in these patterns, in a single sentence:
  1 **as a result of (+ noun) + -ing**
    As a result of the company changing its culture, morale among staff fell.
  2 **as a result of which / with the result that**
    The company culture became more authoritarian and less caring, **as a result of which / with the result that** morale among staff fell.

therefore/consequently

- at the beginning of a second sentence, followed by a comma:
  Key members of staff felt that they were being put under intolerable pressure by their bosses. **Therefore/ Consequently**, many of them left and joined rival firms.

- between clauses later in a second sentence, with commas before and after:
  Key members of staff felt that they were being put under intolerable pressure by their bosses. Many of them left, **therefore/consequently**, and joined rival firms.

thus/thereby

thus

- = therefore, more formal but appropriate for academic writing:
  Reductions in staffing did not also reduce the overall workload. **Thus**, remaining members of staff were put under enormous pressure.

thus/thereby + -ing

- linking a result with its cause:
  Management did not reduce the overall workload, **thus/thereby putting** remaining members of staff under enormous pressure.

which/this + mean that

Staff numbers were reduced, **which meant that** remaining employees had bigger workloads.
Staff numbers were reduced. **This meant that** remaining employees had bigger workloads.
NOTE: 'which' connects two clauses and 'This' connects two sentences.

> **! Danger Zone**
> **Confusing 'so' and 'such'**
>
> **So** is used with an adjective or adverb; **such** is used with a noun or noun phrase.
>
> Systems changed in so short time that employees became confused. ✗
> Systems changed **so rapidly** that employees became confused. ✓
> Systems changed in **such a short time** that employees became confused. ✓

Exercises

1 Correct the following sentences.

1 Unemployment in the region was high that the Government felt obliged to establish an enterprise zone.
2 The digital revolution in broadcast media has led a much wider range of programme choice for the consumer.
3 Accidents in laboratories may result in a lack of supervision.
4 Funding for the arts fell therefore many groups and organisations were unable to continue.
5 Employment opportunities in the sector fell, resulted in increased competition for jobs.
6 Dickens regularly gave talks and readings, thereby increased his fame with the public.

2 Rewrite the sentences, using the words in brackets.

1 Due to investment in small-scale technology such as mobile phone masts, there has been considerable economic growth in the region. (*resulted in*)
2 As both of the town's electronics factories were forced to close during the recession, the only employment opportunities to be found are in the service and public sectors. (*as a result*)
3 The region was recovering from war and consequently medicines were in short supply. (*this meant that*)
4 Riots continued for ten days. As a result, many villages were left in ruins. (*which meant that*)
5 Radiation leaks at the Chernobyl plant were caused by the absence of a confinement shell. (*resulted*)
6 The cause of seasonal Affective Disorder (SAD) seems to be a shortage of sunlight. (*stem*)

30 Signposting

Certain words and phrases act as **signposts** to point your reader to other parts of your essay.

 Writing Tip

A coherent piece of writing works as a whole, rather than as a series or list of separate points.

▶ **Read this paragraph from an essay on international relations and look at the way in which the writer deals with key pieces of information.**

Japan, which has an emperor as head of state, and the United Kingdom, which has a monarch as head of state, are sometimes compared with each other. Japan remained culturally isolated for a long period of its history, while the United Kingdom evolved through its engagements, peaceful and military, with the world. Despite these differences, there are some interesting similarities.

What's wrong: There is too much repetition of information ('which has ... as head of state', 'Japan', 'the United Kingdom').

• Here is the paragraph with three signposting words or phrases:

Japan and the United Kingdom, with an emperor and monarch as head of state **respectively**, are sometimes compared with each other. **The former country** remained culturally isolated for a long period of its history, while **the latter** evolved through its engagements, peaceful and military, with the world. Despite these differences, there are some interesting similarities.

the former, the latter

If you have mentioned two things in your writing and want to refer back to them:

the former → 'the first one mentioned'
the latter → 'the second/last one mentioned'

• 'Former' and 'latter' can act as adjectives or be used alone as nouns. In the paragraph above:
  the former country = Japan
  the latter = the UK

• You can use these phrases together as in the text above, or you can use them on their own:
  In the middle of the 19th century, Japan opened itself to trade and ended its feudal system. **The former** development initially brought chaos, as foreign traders exploited the currency's unrealistic exchange rate between gold and silver. ('the former development' = Japan opening itself to trade)

respectively

means 'in the order in which I mentioned them.' It can be used at the end of a clause or earlier in the sentence:
Japan and the United Kingdom, with an emperor and monarch as head of state **respectively**, are sometimes compared with each other.
'Sevilo' (from Savile Row) and 'nekutai' are, **respectively**, the Japanese words for a Western style business suit and a tie (or necktie).

above and below

You can use **above** to refer to something immediately before or something anywhere before:

The rapid growth in the Sony Corporation during the 1960s can be seen in the graph **above**.

In the part of this essay **above** on political change, it may have been implied that that the transition to a capitalist economy occurred without opposition.

The following expressions can also be used for reference backwards:

- for reference to the part immediately before

  In the preceding section of this report a comparison was made between ...

- for reference to a specific part before

  As we saw in the first three paragraphs / in the opening section of this essay,

- for general reference backwards

  As we have seen, some similarities stem from the fact that ...

You can use **below** to refer to information that comes immediately afterwards or later on in the text:

In the example **below** from Simpson (2007), it is possible to see how communications between the two countries can be misunderstood.

Several of the accounts described **below** of early visits to Japan by English travellers focus on ceremonial aspects of the culture.

The following expressions can also be used for reference forwards:

- reference to the part immediately afterwards:

  In the following paragraph, the expansion of trade between Japan and its neighbours will be discussed.

- reference to a specific part to come:

  As we shall see in the second half of this essay, ...

- general reference forwards:

  As we shall see, there are some distinct differences between ...

 Remember!

Signposting is an important part of making an argument.

▶ See 'Stating the Scope' in **49** *The language of argument*.

Exercises

1 Complete the gaps with the following words:

above, preceding, following, former, latter

1 As we saw in the .... (*following/preceding*) section of this report, Portugal has suffered a decline in its export productivity.

2 Revenue from agriculture and tourism were mainstays in the Spanish economy. Indeed, income from the .... (*latter/former*) source continued to increase as holidaymakers took advantage of package offers. The boom period eventually came to an end, however, as we shall see in the .... (*following/ preceding*) paragraph.

3 As we have seen ...., (*below/above*) a number of factors combined to produce Ireland's financial crisis.

4 Visitors to Greece are attracted by its historical sites and its beaches. The .... (*latter/former*) include ancient temples and Byzantine monasteries.

2 Rewrite the sentences using <u>one</u> of the two options in brackets.

1 In the preceding paragraph, we saw how Milan emerged as one of Italy's most important commercial centres. (*below* or *above*)

2 After Paris, Lyon is the second biggest city in France and Marseille is the third biggest city. (*respectively*)

3 By exploring the statistics in the table that follows, it will be possible to appreciate the scale of Germany's postwar recovery. (*below* or *above*)

4 There is a certain amount of rivalry between Madrid and Barcelona. Madrid is the centre of power, while Barcelona often regards itself as the economic driving force of the country. (*the former... the latter...*)

31 Using pronouns correctly

A pronoun (e.g. **its**, **they**, **this**, **that**, **she**, **them**) is a word that is used instead of a noun or name to refer to people and things.

> A short presentation can be more effective than a long talk, because the audience may lose track of <u>its</u> main point.

The main point of what?

A short presentation?

Or a long talk?

> 💡 **Writing Tip**
>
> Pronouns are widely used for reference purposes and to avoid repeating the same word(s). However, small mistakes can cause significant confusion for your reader.

Using personal pronouns

▶ **Look at these sentences from an essay on EU business activity and try to find the mistakes.**

1. According to the minutes, both partners signed the contract at the same time as the confidentiality agreement, and passed it to the company lawyers. ❌
2. The CEO asked his accounts manager why he had not been notified of the changes in EU regulations. ❌
3. A senior manager is responsible for the actions of their team. ❌

What's wrong: The pronoun references are unclear, confusing or incorrect.

- Here are the sentences with accurate pronoun use:
1. It must be clear what 'it' refers to: *the contract* or *the confidentiality agreement*. Here are two possible ways of doing this:
   According to the minutes, both partners signed the contract at the same time as the confidentiality agreement, and passed **the contract** to the company lawyers. ✔
   According to the minutes, both partners signed the contract at the same time as the confidentiality agreement, and passed **the former** to the company lawyers. ✔
   ▸ See 'the former and the latter' in **30** *Signposting*.

2. It is not clear who 'he' refers to: *the CEO* or *the accounts manager*. Here are two ways of correcting this:
   The CEO asked his accounts manager why he had not **notified him** of the changes in EU regulations. ✔
   The CEO asked his accounts manager why **the latter** had not **notified him** of the changes in EU regulations. ✔

3. The writer has used *their* because the senior manager could be a man or woman. Although this is common in spoken English, it is better to use one of these alternatives in formal English:
   A senior manager is responsible for the actions of **his or her** team. ✔
   Senior managers are responsible for the actions of **their** teams. ✔

this, these, that, those

- *this* and *these* tend to refer to things that are close to us, and *that* and *those* to things that are more distant:
  this argument → the one we are talking about now; **that** argument → the one mentioned earlier
  That argument is no longer accepted by the scientific community.
- *this* is also frequently used on its own to refer to a complete idea:

> Consumer loyalty can be crucial to the success of a brand. **This** is clear from a recent study in The Economist.

- **that + of** and **those + who** are used to mean *the one of* and *the ones who* respectively:

The process of setting objectives is similar to **that** (= **the process**) **of** determining a brand identity.
Retail experts describe two types of consumer: **those** (= **consumers**) **who** know exactly what they are looking for, and **those** (= **consumers**) **who** hope to be inspired by what they see.

- To make clear what idea *this/these* refer back to, it is often necessary to use **this/these + a summarising noun**

The Government plans to support small businesses by cutting some of the bureaucracy that makes it difficult for them to respond quickly to new situations. **This policy** has been welcomed by the CBI.

Nouns that you can use to summarise in this way include:

advice, argument, claim, crisis, criticism, description, development, disagreement, discussion, estimate, example, explanation, idea, increase, issue, measure, objective, phenomenon, policy, problem, proposal, reduction, remark, situation, system, subject, suggestion, trend, view, warning

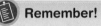 **Remember!**

Don't use 'them' instead of 'those'.
Many people have stopped buying ~~them~~ those goods.

such

- **such a + singular noun** and **such + plural/uncountable noun** mean 'of the kind/type already mentioned':

An impressive headquarters can be a major asset to a business. If **such a building** can be acquired, it may add considerable value to the company brand.

Green business methods can be more expensive than conventional ones, but **such costs/expenditure** can be worthwhile in terms of a company's image.

Exercises

1 Improve the sentences, by replacing the underlined pronouns.

1 Senior managers took their staff to a hotel, where <u>they</u> gave presentations on possible future directions for the company. (NOTE: The senior managers gave the presentations.)
2 To do <u>their</u> job well, a human resources manager needs imagination as well as knowledge of procedures.
3 The conference on performance management ended with a keynote speech. <u>It</u> was a great success, according to those who attended. (NOTE: The keynote speech was a great success.)
4 A council of student representatives was formed at the university, and <u>their</u> task was to represent the views of the student body.

2 Choose the more appropriate options.

1 Several senior managers pointed out the risks if the business expanded too fast. These *explanations/ warnings* were ignored, however, by the CEO.
2 More and more SMEs are seeking business abroad. This *trend/proposal* is a reflection of the lack of opportunities in the UK.
3 Regulations to prevent the import of certain foodstuffs have been put in place at UK borders. These *objectives/measures* are designed to protect public health.
4 A recent study suggests that employees with the same political views as their senior managers are more likely to be promoted. This *system/phenomenon* was, however, first described twenty years ago.

3 Correct any sentences that are wrong.

1 Many managers are unhappy with the criteria on which their performance-related bonuses are based. These who are most critical suggest that conformity rather than creativity is often rewarded.
2 Stellmann plc has introduced mandatory staff drugs testing at their headquarters in Seattle, despite warnings that such measure could result in widespread opposition from employees.
3 Some companies ask staff to appraise their own performance. Recent research has shown such schemes to be relatively successful.
4 The interview process is sometimes compared to those of a lottery.

32 Avoiding repetition of words

There are several ways that you can avoid repetition in your writing:

- by using substitute words such as 'one';
- by omitting unnecessary words;
- by using words/phrases with the same or a similar meaning (synonyms).

> ### 💡 Writing Tip
> Use the techniques outlined in this unit along with those in **30** and **31** to make your writing as clear and coherent as possible.

Substituting words

▶ **Read the sentences below and think about how you could avoid repeating the underlined words.**

Unlike other housing projects in the area, the <u>housing project</u> in Philadelphia evolved through the equal participation of the Mayor's office and the local community.

The charity converted several disused car parks into winter soup kitchens. When it had <u>converted the car parks</u>, it was able to provide daily meals for more 200 people.

It may take homeless people some time to acquire a permanent address, but they can apply for a job more easily by <u>acquiring a permanent address</u>.

- You can use **one(s)** to avoid repeating nouns

Unlike other housing projects in the area, the **one** in Philadelphia …

- In formal writing it is common to avoid repeating a verb phrase by using the appropriate form of **do + so**:

The charity converted several disused car parks into winter soup kitchens. When it had **done so**, it was able to provide daily meals for more than 200 people.

It may take homeless people some time to acquire a permanent address, but they can apply for a job more easily by **doing so**.

Omitting unnecessary words

▶ **Read the sentences below and think about how you could avoid repeating the underlined words.**

Many council workers feel sympathy for homeless members of their community, but few <u>council workers</u> respond to the problem, as Mike Forster did, by setting up a shelter.

There are two short-term solutions to the problem of homelessness. The first <u>solution</u> involves converting empty properties into viable accommodation.

A Government spokesperson praised the schemes that the charity had set up, and some of the most successful <u>schemes</u> were later adopted nationally.

- You can leave out the noun after words such as **both, few, many** and **some**, which describe 'how many':

Many council workers feel sympathy for homeless members of their community, but **few** respond to the problem, as Mike Forster did, by setting up a shelter.

- If the meaning is clear, you can leave out the noun when it follows an adjective:

There are two short-term solutions to the problem of homelessness. The **first** involves converting empty properties into viable accommodation.

A government spokesperson praised the schemes that the charity had set up, and some of the most **successful** were later adopted nationally.

NOTE: In the sentence above, you could also write … 'successful ones were …'

Using synonyms

Synonyms not only help you avoid repetition, they also show that you can think creatively and vary the words that you use.

▶ **Read this paragraph and find the synonyms that the writer uses to avoid repeating the words/phrases in bold.**

Stephen Day, one of the authors of the report on **the hostel**, began working in Liberia as a freelance journalist, but soon became involved in various aid projects. This led to the **setting up** of his own hostel for homeless **boys**. Once established, the house became a refuge for young men who had often run away from abusive fathers. Its success seems to have led from a **combination** of basic discipline and an attempt to bring the boys into the decision-making processes that ran the hostel. Together, these two aspects of the daily life in their new accommodation helped the troubled youths to regain some elements of self-respect.

- Here are the synonyms:
  the hostel → *the house* → *their new accommodation*
  setting up → *established*
  boys → *young men* → *the troubled youths*
  combination → *these two aspects*

- Here is the paragraph with the synonyms in italics:

Stephen Day, one of the authors of the report on **the hostel**, began working in Liberia as a freelance journalist, but soon became involved in various aid projects. This led to the **setting up** of his own hostel for homeless **boys**. Once *established*, *the house* became a refuge for *young men* who had often run away from abusive fathers. Its success seems to have led from a **combination** of basic discipline and an attempt to bring the boys into the decision-making processes that ran the hostel. Together, *these two aspects* of the daily life in *their new accommodation* helped the *troubled youths* to regain some elements of self-respect.

Exercises

1 Amend the sentences to avoid repetition.

1 Most young people make compromises with their parents that allow the family to work as an entity, but some teenagers seem unable to make compromises.
2 The two housing trusts decided to merge in 2009. Both housing trusts believed that working together would improve outcomes.
3 Of all the charities working with homeless people, the charity whose name is most familiar to the public is Shelter.
4 There have been many attempts to renovate empty housing stock and make it available to families in need. The latest attempt has been sponsored by the property group Camden Holdings.
5 Stapleton Ltd agreed in 2006 to improve the living conditions of their 540 tenants in Islington, but when an inspection took place in 2008, it was evident that they had not improved the living conditions.

2 Rewrite this paragraph using synonyms to replace the underlined words.

The charity Homes for People invested some of their savings in a business with a scheme for constructing ecological housing on a site outside Leeds. The site for the scheme seemed ideal, but it became apparent after six months that very little housing was actually being constructed. When the charity contacted the business to establish why six months had elapsed without any obvious progress, they discovered that the entire scheme had been sub-contracted to a smaller business.

33   Parallel structures

Some sentences involve repeating the same grammatical structure to link points. Repeated grammatical forms of this kind are called **parallel structures**.

- There are many different types of parallel structure. Here are some examples:

Sentence	What are the parallel forms?
Television was originally **designed to** educate, (to) amuse **and** (to) entertain the masses. →	The underlined verbs all link back to 'designed to', though it is not necessary to repeat 'to'.
The student was accepted on to the course because **he had** the correct language level **and** (he had) the required school exam results. →	The underlined noun phrases link back to 'he had'. It is not necessary to repeat 'he had'.
The person who gave the presentation **and** (who) designed the website is a friend of mine. →	The underlined verb phrases link back to 'the person who'. It is not necessary to repeat 'who'.

▶ **Read the student's notes from a lecture on the subject of new media. Then read the sentence beside it and underline the parallel structures. What error has the student made?**

Excessive use of new media:

a) affects performance at school

b) influences behaviour at home

c) limits overall attention spans

There is evidence that excessive use of new media among children can affect their performance at school, influence their behaviour at home and limiting their overall attention spans. ✖

What's wrong: Different verb forms are used within the parallel structures. The first two verbs 'affect' and 'influence' are parallel. They are not in the singular form because they go together with 'can'. The third verb should therefore be in the same form as 'affect' as it is also linked with 'can' → 'can limit'.

- Here is the sentence with parallel structures:

  There is evidence that excessive use of new media among children **can affect** their performance at school, **influence** their behaviour at home and **limit** their attention spans. ✔

- Here are some more complex examples of sentences with parallel structures:

Despite spending many hours a day on computer games consoles **and** hardly ever reading, some of the teenagers studied had high reading comprehension skills.

NOTE: 'despite' is followed by the '-ing' form of a verb. 'Reading' is in the same form because this part of the sentence means 'despite hardly ever reading'.

Some experts **recommend that** parents should restrict home computer use **and that** this use should always be supervised by parents.

NOTE: 'that' is repeated because the first underlined section is about 'parents' whereas the second underlined section is about the 'use' of computers. In other words, the subject in each clause is different.

Home computer use **proved** to be a significant factor in performance in tests and to have an influence on behaviour in the classroom.

NOTE: 'to' must be repeated because 'to be' and 'to have' form part of two separate phrases: 'to be a factor in' / 'to have an influence on'.

Neither/nor

This structure is used for expressing two connected negatives but the verbs used are not negative and both of them must be in the same form:

Findings from research into the effects of internet use **are neither consistent nor point** to any major problem. ✓

NOTE: both verbs 'are' and 'point' relate to the subject of the sentence 'findings'

→ Findings are not consistent + Findings do not point

Findings are neither consistent and they don't point…. ✗

Findings aren't neither consistent or point…. ✗

Note also the word order when using 'neither and nor' in this way.

Remember!

When a sentence contains parts that are linked to the same structure, their grammatical form must also be the same (though some words within the structure may be omitted).

Exercises

1 Underline the parallel forms in the sentences.

1 Many companies are using call centres in India to promote products, deal with enquiries and complaints, and monitor consumer behaviour.

2 Unlike humans, animals have an acute sense of smell and, if they need food, know where to find it.

3 As young people spend more and more time on media-based websites, celebrity culture is being blamed for an increase in materialism and a fall in creativity.

4 In some countries, streets have been transformed from car-centred areas to social spaces in which neighbours meet, children play and the car driver is an occasional visitor.

5 Unfortunately, neither using the internet to shop, nor going through a self-service checkout speeds up supermarket shopping.

6 We plan to introduce a new advertising campaign across the country but do not have an immediate timescale for the roll out.

2 Correct/improve the students' sentences by using parallel structures.

1 The course syllabus includes an analysis of the concept of innovation, designing technical images and you will prepare project specifications.

2 The music is entitled 'Before Dawn', which was written by Dominique Ferris and published in 2010.

3 The research will investigate the number of people leaving school early and get married.

4 Equipment has to be bought, laboratories set up and hiring of staff is done before any work can begin.

5 Global air travel is safe, convenience and more efficiency of fuel than it used to be.

6 When you entertain someone from another country, it's hard to decide whether to shake their hand or should you wait and see what they do first.

3 Turn the notes into sentences with parallel structures.

1

> Benefits of team work:
>
> – mix with different personality types
>
> – pooling ideas
>
> – joint decisions

2

> Successful marketing strategy:
>
> – objectives – clear
>
> – advertising campaign (wide-ranging)
>
> – public support – strong

34 Participles

What are participles?

A present participle is a form of a verb ending with -ing → *facing*

A past participle is often a form of a verb ending with -ed → *worked*
Many common past participles do not end in -ed (e.g. *done, driven, known*)

A past participle can also be used after 'having' → *having worked, having done*

> ### 💡 Writing Tip
> Using participles enables you to produce sophisticated sentences that connect important pieces of information. This can be more effective than writing short simple sentences or linking these using simple conjunctions such as 'and' or 'because'.

- You can use participles to

1 describe causes and results

The country's car industry was obliged to restructure in the 1990s because it faced the effects of a recession. →

Facing the effects of a recession in the early 1990s, the country's car industry was obliged to restructure.

2 give important additional information

Exports grew over the next few years. They were driven by an international marketing campaign. →

Exports, **driven** by an international marketing campaign, grew over the next few years.

3 present a sequence of events

Michael Tadakis worked in the travel industry. Then he formed his own company in 2007. →

Michael Tadakis formed his own company in 2007, **having** previously **worked** in the travel industry.

▶ **Read this sentence about shareholders.**

Having gained a 28 per cent market share in the UK, shareholders were very pleased with the company's performance. ✗

What's wrong: The sentence does not make sense. The subject of the participle ('Having gained') is not the same as the subject of the rest of the sentence and the verb 'were'. The shareholders did not gain the market share, the company did.

> ### 📋 Remember!
> The subject of the participle must be the same as the main subject of the sentence as a whole. To illustrate this, the subjects have been underlined in the three examples above.

- The subject should be consistent and be either the shareholders

The UK shareholders were very pleased with the company's performance, having been told that it had gained a 28 per cent market share. ✓

- or the company

Having gained a 28 per cent market share in the UK, the company made a special announcement to delighted shareholders. ✓

Exercises

1 Decide if these sentences are correct or not.

1 Spotting a gap in the market, a new model was launched in 2009.
2 The CEO, having called in a firm of consultants, decided to drastically restructure the company.
3 Written in 1997, he had a huge success with his autobiography.
4 The budget, designed to accommodate some seasonal variation in prices, was still an under-estimate.
5 Having sought the opinions of leading investors, the proposed merger was abandoned.
6 The private sector created a range of new jobs, satisfying the needs of government policy.

2 Write single sentences using participles.

1 They carried out extensive market research. Then they launched the new product.
2 The management wished to streamline the operation. Therefore they reduced staffing.
3 Competitors overtook the company in terms of market share. It had to respond quickly.
4 The garage began to struggle. It was experiencing keen competition from other companies.
5 The officers drew up a shortlist of candidates. Then they passed it to the manager for review.
6 Customer satisfaction rose to an all time high during the holiday period. It was monitored by in-store complaints records.

3 Turn the notes about companies into sentences with participles.

1
> *Jagger PLC:*
>
> *– lost market share*
>
> *– made 100 staff redundant*
>
> *– operated as a smaller company*
>
> *– returned to profitability*

2
> *Bull Construction Ltd:*
>
> *– founded in 2008*
>
> *– grew quickly*
>
> *– landed a major public sector contract in 2009*
>
> *– moved to new premises*

35   Incomplete sentences

Although participants were chosen for the experiment from a wide variety of backgrounds.

What does this mean? Has anyone seen the other part of this sentence?

Writing Tip

Make sure that every sentence you write really is a complete sentence. An incomplete sentence is a serious error that will give the reader a very bad impression of your work.

▶ **Read this extract from a science essay and think about which sentences are complete and which are incomplete.**

The results of the experiment were consistent. Regardless of the background of the subjects. Or the time-frame over which the experiment was conducted. The researchers were therefore able to draw firm conclusions from the experiment. Not that these were universally accepted in the scientific world. Because they contradicted previous research.

What's wrong: The second, third and last sentences are not complete sentences; they are parts of sentences. They all contain words and phrases that link parts of sentences together (*regardless of, or, because*), but they are all clauses that cannot stand alone.

● Here is the extract with complete sentences throughout:

The results of the experiment were consistent, regardless of the background of the subjects or the time-frame over which the experiment was conducted. The researchers were therefore able to draw firm conclusions from the experiment. Not that these were universally accepted in the scientific world, because they contradicted previous research.

● To be complete, a sentence needs to have **a subject and a main verb**. As such, it carries an idea and makes sense on its own.   ▶ See **2** *Parts of a sentence.*

In the first sentence of the correct paragraphs above, 'results' is the subject and 'were' is the main verb.

Extra information

The results of the experiment   were consistent...
⎵⎵⎵⎵⎵⎵⎵⎵⎵⎵⎵   ⎵⎵⎵⎵⎵⎵⎵⎵
     subject   main verb

+   regardless of the background of the subjects.

+   regardless of the time frame over which the experiment was conducted.

The extra pieces of information have no main verb. They are not complete sentences that make sense on their own.

● A complete sentence can begin with a **linking word**, but the sentence then has to have **another clause**:
Because they contradicted a lot of previous research in the area. ✖
This only has one clause and so it does not make sense.

● A complete sentence can begin with a negative word as long as it has a subject and main verb:
Not that **these were** universally accepted in the scientific world. ✔
▶ See **12** *Negative expressions and structures.*
The subject is 'these' and the main verb is 'were accepted'; the sentence could be rewritten as 'These were not universally accepted in the scientific world.'

Remember!

A sentence has to make complete sense on its own. It may refer to something mentioned elsewhere (*this, these,* etc.) but it must have a complete meaning.

● Here are some more examples of incomplete sentences:

Not a very good example of most research in the field. ✖	→	*There is no subject or main verb; this is a phrase, not a sentence.*
Rather than the kind of research which would have widespread applications. ✖	→	*There is no subject or main verb; this presents an alternative, but does not say what it is the alternative to and so makes no sense on its own.*
Hard to say whether the research results are reliable. ✖	→	*This has no main subject or verb; it is more like an informal spoken statement and it is not a grammatically complete sentence. To be complete it must start 'It is … – 'It is hard to say whether the research results are reliable.'*

❗ Danger Zone

Writing in the way you think

You do not always think in complete sentences! Here's what you might think if you were writing an essay:
The experiment was conducted on adults and children. Didn't make any difference. Same results for both groups. Quite a surprise for the researchers. They had expected to find a significant contrast. ✖

Three of these thoughts are incomplete sentences. Here is one way of presenting them in the essay:
The experiment was conducted on adults and children but this made no difference to the results, which were the same for both groups. This was quite a surprise for the researchers, who had expected to find a significant contrast. ✔

Exercises

1 **Decide if these sentences are complete (✔) or incomplete (✖).**

1 In spite of all the changes that had taken place and how much the situation had altered in the intervening years.

2 With the arrival of environmental engineering, approaches to some projects required fresh thinking.

3 Projects achieved by teams without argument are rare.

4 Using statistics to confuse the reader as much as anything else.

5 Supposedly the most successful research and development laboratory in the UK.

6 Hoping for a result before the morning, some of the team went without sleep.

2 **Read these paragraphs and underline the incomplete sentences. Then rewrite the paragraphs so that they contain only complete sentences.**

To do this you may need to add linking devices to join some sentences, create conditional, relative or participle clauses and/or re-word some parts.

1 The jury system is a central plank of the British legal system. A number of critics of it who say that it is outdated. Many cases too complex for ordinary members of the public. The result they feel that juries should not be used any longer.

2 A number of reasons why the ruling party might lose the next election. The state of the economy is probably the top one. Many people are losing their jobs and businesses are unable to attract investment. A growing loss of faith in the government.

3 A backbench MP can rise to prominence. He or she makes an exceptional speech. It's reported in the press. Or by chairing a committee. Particularly when the committee interviews public figures.

4 TV watchers could not believe how many people the protest attracted. Despite one of the wettest days of the year. On every street in the city centre, hundreds of protestors. Carrying slogans and denounced the government's policies.

5 Some politicians have become very rich after holding office. They have been appointed to company boards. They acquired a high profile in office. So they can command high fees for lectures.

36 Avoiding long & disorganised sentences

▶ **Read this sentence from an essay on management systems.**

In a management system such as this, staff become chiefly concerned with pleasing their managers and they get stressed, and they lose focus on the needs of the company and they are unable to carry out core operations in the best possible way, so the system is acting to the detriment of the organisation.

What's wrong: The sentence is garbled, with too much repetition of 'and'. Too many separate pieces of information are given in a single sentence and the reader loses track. Though grammatically correct, the sentence creates a very bad impression.

● Here are two ways of avoiding long and disorganised sentences when presenting a number of connected points and pieces of information.

1 Create two or more sentences, with clear linking, instead of one very long sentence:

In a management system such as this, staff become chiefly concerned with pleasing their managers. **This causes** them to get stressed and to lose focus on the needs of the company. **As a result**, they are unable to carry out core operations in the best possible way. **Therefore**, the system is acting to the detriment of the organisation.

2 Present a coherent list using parallel structures, a colon and semi-colons, and separate this from any further points or information:

A management system such as this has a number of negative effects on staff: **they become** chiefly concerned with pleasing their managers; **they get stressed**; **they lose focus** on the needs of the company; and **they are unable** to carry out core operations in the best possible way. **This means** that the system is acting to the detriment of the organisation.

▶ See **33** *Parallel structures* and **21** *Colons and semi-colons*.

● Here is another example of a long and disorganised sentence:

Sceptics regard management theories as fads that do more harm than good because companies follow each other in jumping on the bandwagon and changing systems so that they conform to the latest management theory but there is no clear evidence that the theory really works and even if it is a good one, it might not work for every organisation.

The sentence contains the following points:
1 the general view of sceptics;
2 what sceptics think companies do;
3 why sceptics think companies shouldn't do that.

This is too much for a single sentence. The three points need to be made in a coherent, **easy-to-read** way. To do this, they need to be clearly separated into their own sentences:

> Sceptics regard management theories as fads that do more harm than good. They believe that companies follow each other in jumping on the bandwagon and changing systems so that they conform to the latest management theory. However, according to the sceptics, there may be no clear evidence that the theory really works and even if it is a good one, it might not work for every organisation.

! Danger Zone

Rambling sentences

If you have written a very long sentence containing a number of points, read it through and ask yourself these questions:

- *Would it be hard to read the sentence aloud in a way that makes clear sense?*
- *Does it have to be read again in order to be understood?*

If the answer is yes, rewrite the sentence in one of the ways suggested above. It is a mistake to think that you have to produce very long sentences in order to write in an academic style.

Exercises

1 Rewrite the following disorganised sentences as two separate sentences.

1 Studies of youth culture in Britain always tend to focus on the 1960s as that is the period when many changes were clearly visible in British society and when the whole subject became a matter of public debate and in fact many of these developments actually began in the 1950s and any study of youth culture should really begin in that decade.

2 Any study of international relations will show that alliances are constantly shifting so that nations who are close allies for a period of time can become enemies when circumstances change and that is why some wars start because a nation's interests have changed and to act in those interests they now oppose a political leader they previously supported.

3 The difference between sociological and journalistic approaches to events is that in the first approach sociologists have to use scientific methods to gather their information unlike journalists who can easily write up information without witnessing the actual event which makes them biased sometimes.

4 Prime Ministers are like senior managers in that they can delegate much of their power to individual departments and focus their energy instead on overall strategy and presentation or they can micro-manage the individual decisions of their department heads but if they choose this route, they risk being overwhelmed by the sheer scale of modern government.

2 Decide whether these sentences are clear or disorganised, and rewrite the disorganised ones as two sentences.

1 The organisation had systems in place that suited it very well at first, but as it grew, these systems proved inadequate and management realised that a complete re-appraisal was required.

2 George Orwell is chiefly known for his novels 'Animal Farm' and 'Nineteen Eighty-Four' and these are still widely read today and he also wrote a great deal of journalism and his journalism is very important, for example 'The Road to Wigan Pier' about the life of miners and the relevance of socialism.

3 The Equality in Employment Act prevents employers from discriminating against a person on the grounds of their age, either by not offering them a job which they are qualified to do or enforcing early retirement against their wishes.

4 It has been argued, with the benefit of graphic anecdotes, that organisations are hampered by health and safety legislation and when individual elements of the law are closely examined, it becomes clear, and there is an exaggerated interpretation by managers causing the problem rather than the code itself.

37 When to use short sentences

Writing Tip

Although you should avoid using one short sentence after another, a short sentence in the right place can have a powerful impact on the reader, highlighting a key point that might otherwise get lost in a longer sentence.

▶ **Read this paragraph from an essay on urban planning.**

Reactions to the building of tower blocks were initially very mixed because although some people agreed that they provided much-needed housing in urban areas, others complained that they blocked daylight from the streets and could feel rather over-bearing.

What's wrong: The sentence is grammatically correct but the main point that the writer wants to make fails to stand out.

I can't see the wood for the trees

● Here is the same information with the main point presented in a short sentence:

Reactions to the building of tower blocks were initially very mixed. Although some people agreed that they provided much-needed housing in urban areas, others complained that they blocked daylight from the streets and could feel rather over-bearing.

● Read this paragraph from an essay on architecture and planning in Britain, and think about places in it where short sentences would be better:

During the 1950s, there was a great deal of debate about the way that planning and building should go, and in this debate there were two sides with very different views, one of them being the modernists. They were passionate in their belief that modernism was the only option, and that what was needed was the creation of large numbers of high-rise blocks in cities and that this would improve standards of living for those at the lower levels of society. Against them were pitted a range of people who feared the social consequences of high-rise building and the likely destruction of local communities that it would bring with it, but it was the modernists who won the argument.

● Here is the paragraph with short sentences where appropriate:

During the 1950s, there was a great deal of debate about the way that planning and building should go. **(1) In this debate there were two sides with very different views. (2) One of them was the modernists.** They were passionate in their belief that modernism was the only option, and that what was needed was the creation of large numbers of high-rise blocks in cities. **(3) They believed that this would improve standards of living for those at the lower levels of society.** Against them were pitted a range of people who feared the social consequences of high-rise building and the likely destruction of local communities that it would bring with it. **(4) However, it was the modernists who won the argument.**

The four short sentences highlight the key points:

1 the fact that there were two sides in the debate

2 the fact that one group was the 'modernists'
The rest of the paragraph is mainly about the modernists, so it is important to introduce them by using the short sentence.

---

3 the main view of the modernists

Breaking the longer sentence up makes the view clearer. The first sentence now says what they wanted and the second sentence tells the reader why they wanted it.

4 who won the argument

The short final sentence emphasises the point about who won the debate, which is very important information. In the longer sentence, this was presented only as an additional point rather than a main point.

! Danger Zone

Failure to direct your reader

If your focus is obscured, your main points will not stand out.

The policy of creating high-rise estates for working class people continued for many years but there was a widespread feeling that those who created them did not understand what life would be like for the people who had to live in them and many of those people were soon complaining about isolation and social breakdown. ✖

The reader doesn't know what the main point is here because the writer is trying to say too much in a single sentence.

The policy of creating high-rise estates for working class people continued for many years. However, there was a widespread feeling that those who created them did not understand what life would be like for the people who had to live in them. **Many of those people were soon complaining about isolation and social breakdown.** ✔

📋 Remember!

Short sentences can often be the best way of presenting main points and drawing attention to important information. For this reason, they often work well at the beginning or end of the paragraph.

Exercises

1 **Isolate the main point in the texts below by creating a short sentence, and making any other necessary changes.**

   1 Much of the housing in east London had been destroyed in the war and much of what remained could be categorised as slums, and something had to be done, therefore a policy of rebuilding in the affected areas was devised and this involved the creation of many high-rise estates.

   2 Under the 1947 law owners no longer had full rights over their land, with final permission for development instead passing to local authorities who were given powers not only to approve new proposals, but also to 'list' buildings of architectural interest, and thus protect them permanently from development.

   3 New buildings can contrast significantly with the landscape around them, providing an interesting element of shock value, or they may blend in harmoniously, so that their presence is hardly noticed, but they must take their surroundings into full account.

2 **Rewrite this paragraph using short sentences where appropriate.**

   As the building programme in many British cities continued in the 1950s and 1960s, opinions as to its effects differed. There were many who felt that it represented a necessary improvement, raising the standards of living of a great many people and transforming these cities into modern ones worthy of the modern age, but other people were far less enthusiastic, and these included many of the people actually living in this new housing. They felt that it had been created by people who would never have to live in it and who had little or no knowledge of how their theories would impact on the residents.

38 Avoiding too many short sentences

 Writing Tip

A short sentence can be preferable to a long one. However, too many short sentences can create confusion and a bad impression, especially if they follow each other.

▶ **Read this extract from an essay on cinema.**

Orson Welles was a prodigy in the world of film. He directed 'Citizen Kane' at the age of 26. He starred in it too. Many people think it is the greatest film ever made. That was in 1941. He made a number of other films then. Some of them are considered masterpieces as well.

What's wrong: The information is given in a series of short and simple sentences. It reads like notes and does not flow. Some of the sentences need to be joined together, using appropriate ways of linking.

● Here is the extract with the sentences linked together:

Orson Welles was a prodigy in the world of film. In 1941, at the age of 26, he directed and starred in 'Citizen Kane', considered by many people to be the greatest film ever made. He subsequently made a number of other films, some of which are considered masterpieces as well.

● Linking parts of sentences may involve:

1 putting related short pieces of information (e.g. dates, numbers, etc.) together, using **commas**:
  In 1941, at the age of 26, he ...

2 putting related facts together to form one part of a sentence, using **linking words**:
  ... he **directed and starred in** 'Citizen Kane'...

3 joining parts of a sentence with **participles**:
  ... 'Citizen Kane', **considered** by many people to be ...
  ◆ See **34** *Participles.*

4 joining parts of a sentence with **relative clauses**:
  ... a number of other films, **some of which are** considered ...
  ◆ See **15** *Relative clauses.*

● Here is another example of a series of short sentences that should be linked:

Citizen Kane' is about the life of a fictional newspaper owner. His name is Charles Foster Kane. The character is based on William Randolph Hearst. He was a US newspaper owner. He was very famous at the time. He didn't like the film. He banned any mention of it in his newspapers. The story is told mostly through flashbacks. A reporter tries to find out why Kane's dying word is 'Rosebud'.

The extract contains information on the following:
1 Kane,
2 Hearst,
3 Hearst's reaction,
4 the content of film.

> **Remember!**
> Before you start writing, it may be a good idea to make brief notes of what you are going to include and then think of ways of joining your ideas together to produce sentences that have an appropriately academic style.

- For each of these things, the information can be linked as follows:

'Citizen Kane' is about the life of a fictional newspaper owner, **whose name** is Charles Foster Kane. The character is based on William Randolph Hearst, **a US** newspaper owner **who** was very famous at the time. He didn't like the film **and banned** any mention of it in his newspapers. **Told** mostly through flashbacks, the film shows a reporter trying to find out why Kane's dying word is 'Rosebud'.

NOTE: The writer uses commas, relative clauses, a participle and a linking word in this version.

! Danger Zone

Focusing only on the information, not the presentation

Before you start writing, think about these issues:

- *How can I group information/points in a longer sentence?*
- *How can I connect information/points within those longer sentences?*

When you have finished writing, polish your sentences, particularly if you did not have time to do this when you were writing them. Think about these issues:

- *How can I forge better links between sentences?*
- *How can I tighten the information?*

If you use some thinking time and the linking methods described in this unit, you can avoid producing work that is too simplistic in its sentence formations.

Exercises

1 Turn these short sentences into one longer sentence by using relative and participle clauses and linking words. You may need to delete, add or move some words.

1 The silent film era began in the late 19th century. It continued until the 1920s. Then recorded sound became possible.

2 Politicians have become more and more reliant on focus groups. They came into existence in the 1990s. They involve groups of people giving their views on political issues. They are carefully selected.

3 Large hospitals can be cost effective. They can move staff members to an area of greater need. These staff members are underemployed in their part of the building.

4 A small restaurant may have ambitions to expand. It can decide to make an offer on adjacent premises. This way it gains the additional space it requires.

5 The research team was initially criticised for making slow progress. They were actually involved in a fundamental re-thinking of domestic heating systems. This would lead to an innovative and successful design.

2 Using the same methods as in Exercise 1, create two long sentences from these short sentences.

1 The Industrial Revolution transformed the entire world. It could be said to have started in Derbyshire and Shropshire. They are two adjacent counties in the north Midlands. Arkwright's Wheel was invented in Derbyshire in 1771. It used water power for the spinning of cotton. The Iron Bridge in Shropshire was built in 1781. It was the first arch bridge made of cast iron.

2 Michael Cimino submitted a script for 'Heaven's Gate' in 1971. When he submitted it to United Artists, it was called 'The Johnson County War'. The project failed to attract high-profile actors. It was shelved for some time. The film finally began shooting in 1979. It had a budget of $11.6 million. In the end it cost $30 million.

39   Building successful long sentences

The ability to write successful long sentences is one of the key requirements of academic writing.

> 💡 **Writing Tip**
>
> Complex ideas and points require complex sentences. To write in an academic style, you sometimes need to be able to produce long sentences that have two, three or even four parts. These sentences need to make clear sense and be well controlled.

▶ **Look at these ideas for part of an essay on the newspaper industry and think about how they could all be put together into one long sentence.**

| 1990s, arrival of internet | → | newspapers produced online versions | → | negative effect on sales of print papers | → | online version free | → | result: financial problems |

- Focus first of all on the first and last points, and always keep in mind how this long sentence will end. In this case, it will end with a reference to a bad outcome (financial problems) of the first point (the arrival of the internet), which will begin the sentence. This gives you an overall idea of the shape of your sentence:

  arrival of internet → financial problems

> 📋 **Remember!**
>
> When constructing a long sentence, always keep in mind how it is going to end, and build towards that ending.

- Now consider the points between the beginning and the end. The second point describes a response to the first point and the third point describes the result of that:

  1990s, arrival of internet → newspapers produced online versions → negative effect on sales of print papers

- These three points can be linked together to produce a coherent sentence that is complete in meaning:

  In the 1990s, newspapers responded to the arrival of the internet by producing online versions of their papers, which had a negative effect on sales of the print versions.

  This is a perfectly good sentence, quite long but not too long, with two parts linked by 'which' to refer to the situation and action described in the first part.

- Now consider the last two points. The last point describes the result of the fourth point:

  online version free → result: financial problems

- These two points can be linked together to produce a coherent sentence that is complete in meaning:

  Since the online version was free, the result was financial problems for those papers.

  Again, this is a perfectly good sentence on its own, using the linking word 'since' to connect the cause and the result. However, the second sentence can be linked to the first to build a longer sentence that makes clear sense. The points in the second sentence are closely linked to points in the first.

- Here is the complete sentence, covering all five points:

  In the 1990s, newspapers responded to the arrival of the internet by producing online versions of their papers, which had a negative effect on sales of the print versions and, since the online version was free, resulted in financial problems for those papers.

  The last part is linked by 'and' and the verb 'resulted' links with 'which' earlier in the sentence.

- Here is another example of how a successful long sentence can be built, with inter-connecting points linked to produce a coherent whole:

| Online news: | → | welcomed by many, not necessarily by professional journalists | → | view of professional journalists: careers threatened | → | 'amateurs' willing to get little or no money |

Online news has been welcomed by many, but not necessarily by established professional journalists, who see their careers threatened by people they regard as 'amateurs' because they are willing to supply articles for news and review websites for little or no money.

- The first point is linked by 'but' to contrast the reactions →

- the second point is linked to the first by 'who' because the sentence continues to be about professional journalists →

- the last point is linked to the second by 'because' as it explains why the word 'amateurs' is used.
  The sentence is a long one, consisting of four parts, but it has a coherent meaning as a whole because of the way the points are joined, presenting both a view on a particular subject and the reason for that view.
  ▶ See 'Comma splicing' in **20** *Commas 2 – incorrect uses.*

! Danger Zone

Losing control of long sentences

Keep re-reading your sentence as you are writing it. Make sure that each part of it relates to the other parts in a meaningful way.

Political blogs are a good example of how online journalism can have a significant influence *even though only a small number of people read them, they are often key decision-makers and so* **these blogs can have a serious impact on political debate.** ✖

The beginning and end are fine and make a clear point, but the sentence becomes incoherent and ungrammatical in the middle.

Political blogs are a good example of how online journalism can have a significant influence even though only a small number of people read them, because the people who do read them are often key decision-makers, and so these blogs can have a serious impact on political debate. ✔

Exercise

Write one long sentence that includes all of the points and information in the notes. You will need to use a grammatical elements such as linkers, relative pronouns and parallel structures.

1 Sports psychology:
   based on belief many top competitors of similar ability
   winners/losers separated by state of mind
   also by ability to meet mental challenge not just physical one

2 1990s:
   significant in country's development
   economy grew faster than ever before
   number of social changes
   result: various problems

3 Long-term storage of files:
   easy to access and requiring little storage space
   data is still present years or decades later
   danger: machine malfunction makes it unreadable
   problem: spare parts no longer available

40   Generalising

▶ **Read this sentence from a report on a new medical treatment and consider the meaning and the tone in which it is conveyed.**

It is accepted that the new treatment should be made available to the public as soon as possible.

● Here is the same sentence with a less assertive tone. The writer generalises in order to show an awareness that some people may have a different view.

It is **generally** accepted that the new treatment should be made available to the public as soon as possible.

● Ways of generalising include:

1 using phrases connected with the word 'general'

The treatment proved **generally** effective, with many patients showing significant improvement.
In general (terms), the treatment was effective, though not all patients showed significant improvement.

2 using other phrases that mean 'generally'

On the whole, the treatment proved effective, with many patients showing significant improvement.
By and large, the treatment was effective, though not all patients showed significant improvement.

3 referring to most people/objects, rather than all

The majority of patients responded well to the treatment, although some experienced unpleasant side effects.
The treatment was effective **in most cases**, though some patients experienced unpleasant side effects.

4 using 'tend' and 'tendency'

The side effects **tended** to involve a mild headache or stomach upset.
There **was a tendency for** the side effects to be minor and short-lived.
Younger patients **had a tendency to** ignore the side effects.

▶ **Here are some more examples of where to use these phrases in a sentence. Compare them with the examples above.**

Generally, the treatment proved effective, with many patients showing significant improvement.

The treatment was effective **in general (terms)**, though not all patients showed significant improvement.

The treatment proved effective **on the whole**, with many patients showing significant improvement.

The treatment was effective **by and large**, though not all patients showed significant improvement.

Although some patients experienced unpleasant side effects, **the majority** responded well.

Though some patients experienced unpleasant side effects, **in most cases** the treatment was effective.

The side-effects **tended not to be** long-lasting.

Ignoring the side effects was a common **tendency** in some trial groups.

! Danger Zone

Over-assertive statements

Think about whether what you are saying is completely true or only generally true.

People who exercise regularly stay healthier than people who do not.

Is this statement 100 per cent true for everyone? It is better to make clear that this is a generalisation:

In general, people who exercise regularly stay healthier than people who do not.

Exercises

1 Which of these statements are only generally true? Rewrite them in two different ways so that the tone is less assertive.

1 Obesity is the result of over-eating.
2 Parents immunise their children against childhood diseases.
3 Different countries have different healthcare systems.
4 Children eat more junk food nowadays than in the past.
5 Medical treatment in Britain is funded through taxation.
6 Supermarkets in Britain sell a range of pharmaceutical products.

2 Use the word in brackets to generalise.

1 There is concern that antibiotics are losing their effectiveness. (*tending*)
2 Attempts to educate the public about the need to adopt healthier lifestyles have been successful. (*terms*)
3 The system of health care currently in operation works well. (*whole*)
4 Patients trust their doctors' opinions. (*tendency*)
5 Children suffer from more coughs and colds than adults. (*general*)
6 Experts were surprised that the treatment failed to work. (*cases*)
7 The trial report noted that the tablets relieved symptoms. (*majority*)
8 People who exercise don't get ill as often as people who have sedentary lifestyles. (*tend*)

3 Improve this paragraph by rewriting the underlined sections so that they have a less assertive tone.

When antibiotics were first developed, they completely changed the face of medicine. <u>Illnesses that used to be fatal,</u> could suddenly be cured with a simple course of pills. Unfortunately, the long-term outcome has been that <u>people over-rely on them and doctors over-prescribe them</u>. What does this mean for the future? Unless scientists continue to produce new antibiotics, the ones we depend on today <u>will no longer be effective</u>.

41 Qualifying a statement

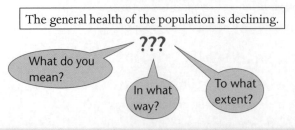

The general health of the population is declining.

???

What do you mean?

In what way?

To what extent?

'**In terms of** exercise and diet, the general health of the population is declining.'

💡 Writing Tip

When presenting an argument or claim, it is important that the reader understands clearly the particular way in which you think it is true. By doing this, you avoid making empty generalisations that lead to unanswered questions.

▶ **There are various ways that you can qualify a statement.**

1 by using phrases that show there are/were other reasons for an outcome
- Read this sentence from a health report: Health improvements have resulted from lifestyle changes.
- Here are two versions of the same sentence, showing that lifestyle changes were not the only reason for health improvements:

To some extent, health improvements resulted from lifestyle changes.
Health improvements resulted **to a/some degree** from lifestyle changes.

2 by using phrases that explain in what way something is true

Lifestyle changes led to health improvements, **in the sense that** they made people less susceptible to minor ailments.
To the extent that they made people less susceptible to minor ailments, lifestyle changes led to improvements.
In that they alleviated some of the symptoms of the illness, lifestyle changes were effective.
Lifestyle changes were effective, **insofar as** they alleviated some of the symptoms of the illness.

3 by using phrases that clarify which aspect of the statement is true

Lifestyle changes led to health improvements, **with regard to** people's susceptibility to minor ailments.
In terms of health improvements, lifestyle changes had a greater impact than regular medical check-ups.

◗ See **17** *Describing similarities and differences.*

📋 Remember!

These words and phrases can be used in different parts of sentences. You can use them to start sentences, to join different parts of a sentence or within parts of a sentence.

▶ **Here are some more examples of where to use these phrases in a sentence. Compare them with the examples above.**

Health improvements resulted **to some extent** from lifestyle changes.
Health improvements resulted from lifestyle changes **to a/some degree**.
In the sense that they made people less susceptible to minor ailments, lifestyle changes led to health improvements.
Lifestyle changes led to health improvements, **to the extent that** they made people less susceptible to minor ailments.
Lifestyle changes were effective **in that** they alleviated some of the symptoms of the illness.
Insofar as they alleviated some of the symptoms of the illness, lifestyle changes were effective.

With regard to people's susceptibility to minor ailments, lifestyle changes had a significant impact. Lifestyle changes had a greater impact, **in terms of** health improvements, than regular medical check-ups.

▶ **There are also ways to show that you accept a statement may not be completely true.**

Patients with a positive outlook on life will recover more quickly than other patients.

'**It seems quite possible that** patients with a positive outlook on life will recover more quickly than others.'

1 by using verbs like *seem* and *appear*

It seems that mental attitude contributes to a person's recovery rate.
Mental attitude **appears** to contribute to a person's recovery rate.

2 by using probability language like *likelihood, likely, probable, possible, possibility*

It is highly probable that patients who live alone will take longer to recover from an accident than those who live in families.
Children are **more likely** to make a complete recovery from this illness than adults.
There is a (strong) possibility that the initial diagnosis was incorrect.

3 using tentative phrases, such as *it could be argued that, it may be that*

It **could be argued** that a hospital is not the best place for some patients to be.
When discussing patient care, **it may be that** a government review is what is required.

> **! Danger Zone**
> **Giving insufficient information**
>
> The rehabilitation programme was not a success.
> In what way was it 'not a success'? Did it fail completely? More information is needed:
> The rehabilitation programme was not a success **in that** the patient failed to make sufficient progress over the two-month period.

Exercises

1 Qualify each statement in a single sentence, using the words in brackets.

1 The public health campaign was successful. It raised awareness of the issue. (*to the extent that*)
2 The treatment was effective. It alleviated some of the symptoms for a period of time. (*insofar as*)
3 Exercise is important. It can, according to research, facilitate mental health. (*in that*)
4 The advertising campaign worked. It removed some of the stigma attached to sexually-transmitted diseases. (*in the sense that*)

2 Rewrite these sentences using the words in brackets without changing them.

1 People who take no exercise and eat a great deal of junk food will become obese. (*likely*)
2 Patients require years of support to recover fully from post-traumatic stress disorder. (*seem*)
3 High levels of stress at work will lead to illness. (*probable*)
4 Alcohol abuse plays a significant part in domestic violence. (*appears*)
5 Drug rehabilitation schemes have reduced levels of addiction in inner-city areas. (*to some extent*)

3 Amend this text to show that the statements may not be completely true.

The latest research indicates that poor diet is a contributing factor in a number of serious illnesses. The Government should therefore increase the amount of money it spends on education programmes. Improving the nation's diet will prove cost effective in terms of the money it will save the National Health Service. Fewer ill people will also represent a saving to business in terms of a reduction in sick leave.

42   Giving a definition

This sentence gives a definition of the term 'communications protocol'.

→

> In computing, **a communications protocol** is the system of rules which allows computers to exchange messages.

> ### 💡 Writing Tip
> It is often necessary to give a clear definition of a word or phrase you are using so that the reader knows exactly what you mean by it.

▶ **Here are some ways of giving a definition.**

- **term** (the thing you are defining) + **be** + **category** (the wider group) + **a relative clause**

    term   be   category   relative clause

  An optical fibre is a telecommunications cable which is made of glass.

- Here is another example:

    term   be   category   relative clause

  Morse code is a form of communication which uses long and short sounds or flashes of light.

> ### ❗ Danger Zone
> **Leaving out the category noun**
>
> Don't leave out the category noun when you refer to the term for the first time:
>
> A spectrograph separates an incoming wave into a frequency spectrum. ❌
>
> A spectrograph **is an instrument that** separates an incoming wave into a frequency spectrum. ✅

- **using different category nouns**

  1 The category nouns **means, method, process** and **technique** are often followed by **whereby** or **by which:**

  > Nonverbal communication is the **means by which/whereby** messages are conveyed visually rather than by words.

  2 The category nouns **device, implement, instrument, machine, mechanism** and **tool** are often followed by **for + -ing:**

  > A transmitter is an electronic **device for producing** radio waves.

> ### 📋 Remember!
> Your definition needs to be more than an example – it needs an explanation.
>
> A social networking site is an online platform such as Facebook, which has more than 800 million users. ❌
>
> A social networking site is an online platform (such as Facebook) that seeks to bring people and their interests into contact with each other. ✅

● **using different verbs**

Two group of verbs are regularly used in definitions:

1 describe, mean, refer to, signify

Sentences with these verbs sometimes start with 'The term...' or 'The word ...':

The term 'multiplexing' **describes** communication between more than two parties or devices.

2 be defined as, be known as, be called

If you are using a quotation or paraphrasing from a dictionary or another source, you can use **be + defined as**:

Lobbying **is defined** by Semeraro **as** the attempt to influence the policy decisions of legislators or government agencies.

If you are making your own definition, use **can/could/may/might + be + defined as**:

Propaganda **could be defined as** a form of communication that tries to influence the views of a community through biased information.

Use **be + known as** and **be + called** when you put the term at the end of the sentence:

A collection of people who come together to seek to influence public policy **is known as/is called** an advocacy group.

> 📋 **Remember!**
>
> You can give a short definition within a longer sentence by using commas or brackets:
>
> All the studios contain at least one isolation booth (a small room with extra soundproofing).
> All the studios contain at least one isolation booth, a small room with extra soundproofing.

Exercises

1 Improve or correct these definitions.

1 An avatar can be defined by Spinrad in 'Songs from the Stars' (1980) as a representation of a human that allows him or her to participate in a virtual world.
2 A digital immigrant is a person was born before the start of the digital age.
3 Data mining is a process which a company develops profiles of potential customers through information collated from their online behaviour.
4 A computer virus is a program such as the Conficker worm, which attacked British and French defence systems in 2008.
5 Apple Inc. produces and sells consumer electronics, personal computers and computer software.
6 A mouse is a process for controlling the movement of a cursor on a computer screen.

2 Write definitions of these terms in your own words.

1 Cyber bullying
2 Wikipedia
3 Globalisation
4 A USB flash drive
5 A chat room

43   Introducing an example

This sentence gives an example of a modern farming method that has been under discussion.

→

For some time now, there has been <u>considerable discussion</u> about modern farming methods. The <u>debate</u> over the use of pesticides is **just one example**.

> ### Writing Tip
> When introducing an example, it is important to make a clear and accurate link between your main argument or claim and the information you are using to support it.

▶ **Read this sentence from a report on modern farming methods.**

Government control affects many areas of farming and farmers often suffer as a result: e.g. farm management. ✖

What's wrong: The example is not clearly linked to the main argument and it has been incorporated into the sentence in an ungrammatical way.

● Here is the same sentence with the example clearly and accurately integrated:

Government control affects many areas of farming and farmers often suffer as a result. **An example of this can be seen** in the current approaches to farm management. ✔

● Ways of introducing examples include:

1 using the word 'example'

The general public have had a significant impact on farming practice. **A good example of this is** the pressure that has been mounted over the decades to minimise the battery farming of chickens.

2 using the phrases 'for example' or 'for instance'

There are factors other than the weather that affect the livelihood of farmers. **For example/For instance**, government policies are also highly influential.

3 using 'such as' (particularly for lists)

Many factors, **such as** the weather, government policy and public demand, affect the way farms are run.

4 using phrases connected with the word 'illustrate'

Disagreement over the meaning of 'sustainable agriculture' **is illustrated by** the difference between the government's definition of it and that of many farmers.

> ### Remember!
> The language that you use to speak can be very different from the language that you use to write. Expressions such as *like*, *you know* and *I mean*, which are informal expressions often used to give examples, should never be used in written work for this purpose.

▶ **Here are some more examples of where to use these phrases in a sentence. Compare them with the sentences above.**

There are many farming myths. **Take, for example**, organic farming, which is supposed to be more environmentally friendly. Many people would argue……

Public pressure **is just one example of** the many forces that can be exerted on farming practice.

Just one event can destroy a harvest – a severe tropical storm, **for instance**.

An illustration of the type of misinformation that reaches the public domain is the insistence that small-scale farming is less productive than large-scale farming.

ⓘ Danger Zone

'E.g.' and 'i.e.'

e.g. and i.e. are abbreviations of Latin terms.

e.g. means 'for example'   i.e. means 'that is'

▶ **Look at this sentence:**

Types of farming (e.g. crop rotation and monoculture) will be compared.

This means that many types of farming will be compared; crop rotation and monoculture are examples of these. Without the brackets it is written like this:

Types of farming, e.g. crop rotation and monoculture, will be compared.

▶ **Now look at this sentence:**

The types of farming most common in the region (i.e. crop rotation and monoculture) will be compared.

This means that crop rotation and monoculture are the only types of farming in the region.

The abbreviation 'i.e.' is used for explaining what has been mentioned before. Do not use it for giving examples.

NOTE: Some tutors may prefer you not to use these abbreviations. Check whether your tutor or university has a policy on their use.

Exercises

1 Underline the information that is being exemplified.

1 **An illustration of** just how difficult it can be to pump groundwater can be seen in some coastal areas, where development has been complicated by the contamination of seawater.

2 A range of educational activities can take place on farms, which may even boost income. **Examples of this** can be seen across the country in the 'farm visits' that have been set up for schoolchildren.

3 The increasing population has led to growth in agriculture but this has resulted in a number of complications. The destruction of animal habitats **is one example**.

4 Many laws are designed to protect waterways and land from degradation; **for example**, the Water Resources Act of 1991, which carries a hefty fine for water pollution.

5 Technology has taken over many traditional approaches to enhancing crop performance, **such as** the monitoring of weed growth and irrigation systems.

2 Decide whether these sentences are correct or not. Make any necessary changes.

1 This can improve many people's quality of life like by enabling them to have a better diet.

2 There are many ways to protect plants. Take for example, pesticides.

3 Some developing countries (i.e. in South America and Africa) rely heavily on income from farming.

4 Some statistics on organic farming can be surprising, for example, sugar cane.

5 The decision to expand coffee-growing regions was an illustration of the impact of consumer demand on agricultural decision-making.

6 Assistance to developing countries, such as the provision of technical equipment and know-how, has not always brought about the intended economic advantages.

3 Insert the missing words.

1 Australia is an ...... of a country that has vast areas of organic farmland.

2 There have been many changes in agricultural practice. .... for example the huge increase in organic agricultural land over the past decade.

3 Some crops, ... as cereals, are more widely grown than others around the globe.

4 The public's desire to purchase fresh produce is clearly ...... by the growing support for small-scale farms and their produce.

5 .... example of tried-and-trusted piece of farm equipment is the tractor.

44   Citing

Writing Tip

Citations that are accurately incorporated into your writing strengthen your arguments and significantly enhance the overall impact of what you say.

Sources that are referred to in a piece of writing must be **cited** in an appropriate way, using correct grammar.

▶ Look at the source below, and the student's sentence on the topic of child development:

Source	Student
Despite the existence of pre-school education and the efforts that working parents put into finding the 'best' schools for their children, the family home has the greatest impact on educational development. This can clearly be seen when you look at the studies… *Child Development*, Rogers and Green, 2008	*Rogers and Green (2008) quote:* *'the family home has the greatest* *impact on educational development.'* ✖

What's wrong: The citation has been incorporated into the sentence in an ungrammatical way.

• Here are some correct ways of incorporating citations:

1   **author(s) + date in brackets + verb** (e.g. *argue, point out, state suggest, insist, assert*) **+ that**:

Rogers and Green (2008) argue that 'the family home has the greatest impact on educational development'.

2   **as + author(s) + date in brackets + verb** (e.g. *state, show, demonstrate, point out*) **+ colon** + quote:

As Rogers and Green (2008) point out: 'the family home has the greatest impact on educational development'.

3   **according to + author(s) + date in brackets + comma** + quote:

According to Rogers and Green (2008), 'the family home has the greatest impact on educational development'.

4   **by mentioning the source first**:

In their paper, 'Child Development' (2008), Rogers and Green state that 'the family home has the greatest impact on educational development'.

5   **by rephrasing the view and adding the author(s) + date in brackets at the end of the sentence**:

A child's educational progress is most influenced by their home life (**Rogers and Green, 2008**).

▶ See **46** *Paraphrasing*.

• Here are some more examples of citations. Compare them with the examples above.
   In his famous book 'Circle Game', Minton (2009) drew attention to the need for 'specialised centres'.
   As Peacock and Tramer argue: 'nothing holds back a child more than inattention.'
   Klein, in his paper 'Nothing to Lose' (1999), gives an example of a successful classroom exercise.
   The method lost credibility when parents noticed signs of regression in their children (Packam, 2004).
   Thomas et al (2003) refute this theory, stating that 'studies consistently show that the logic is flawed'.
   Like many earlier experts, Quimper is of the view that 'childhood is our only stage of innocence'.

▶ See 'Quoting' in **24** *Inverted commas*.

Tenses in citations

- When the citation is being used to support a current view or your own view, the **Present Simple** tense or the **Present Perfect** tense are most commonly used.

  Thomas *et al.* (2008) **clearly identify** the areas of need. As they rightly **state**, these are 'on our own doorstep'. Experiments by Greenstein *et al.* (2009, 2010) **have demonstrated** the importance of interactive play.

- You can use the **Past Simple** tense to refer back to a past source that was important at the time.

  Capstan (1965) **defined** the activity as a 'two-tiered initiative'; a term that is still used today.

  Piaget (1896–1980) **established** four stages in child development.

  Jo and Singh (2007) **conducted** a key experiment on identical twins in 2001.

Exercises

1 **Decide whether these citations have been introduced into each sentence correctly. Correct those that are wrong.**

   1 As Jennings states that 'The home is of paramount importance because this is where a child's most basic needs must be met'.
   2 No one really knew what term to use, until Mo (1995) comes up with the expression, 'blue hour'.
   3 Special Needs Education, as Pil and Grew (2007) note, is a growing area of concern.
   4 Barton (2008) quotes that few people really understand the problem.
   5 Green *et al.* argues that price is always a factor.
   6 According to Nudrun *et al.* (2008), television can be a useful educational tool.
   7 In his paper, 'Giving and Receiving', 2006, Jameson explains his theory.
   8 According to Pine-Smith (1975) argues, 'we have to take into account the child's home environment'.

2 **Correct the punctuation (brackets, inverted commas, commas, full stops) in these citations. Two sentences are correct.**

   1 Given sufficient support, children thrive in school (Kinnock and Peters, 2007).
   2 Compliance is a critical factor (Peters 2003 and Lilley 1999).
   3 This behaviour has been examined in a number of works (Johnson 1996; Coates 1998; Green 1999; Kitty 2005).
   4 While nobody can challenge this idea, 'other areas of a child's life also play their part (Fielding 2004).'
   5 Grahams (2006) insists that 'this old notion has to be rejected once and for all.

45 Incorporating data

During your studies, you will come across various types of **data** in a range of formats. Here are some examples:

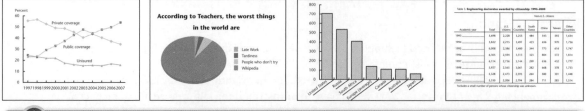

💡 Writing Tip

Whether you are reporting your own data or using a source, the information must be clearly and accurately incorporated into your writing, using appropriate vocabulary.

▶ **Read this paragraph from an essay about research into shopping habits and think about how the vocabulary could be improved.**

The study, performed by a marketing research team, was created to find out information about people's buying habits. A general group of approximately 100 shoppers were interviewed over a four-week period. During this time a lot of data was assembled and checked. Prior to the study, the research team had thought that there would be many differences in the subjects' approach to purchasing. The results showed they were right. They discovered that men spent much more time than women researching their purchases on the internet. However, women shopped more often and spent more overall. These results are the same as those of other similar studies.

What's wrong: The vocabulary is not precise enough. There are certain words and phrases that are commonly used to describe data and many of them have not been used.

● Here is the extract with more appropriate vocabulary.

The study, **conducted** by a marketing research team, was **designed** to **gather** information about people's buying habits. The team interviewed a **random selection** of approximately 100 **participants** over a four-week period. During this time, **a large amount of data** was **collected** and **analysed**. Prior to the study, the team had **predicted** that there would be **considerable variation** in the subjects' approach to purchasing. The results **confirmed** their **expectations**. They **found** that men spent **significantly more** time than women researching their purchases on the internet. However, women shopped **more frequently** and spent **larger sums of money** overall. These **findings** are **consistent with** those of other similar studies.

● Here are some guidelines for describing data:

1 use appropriate verbs and verb forms

The study, **conducted** by a marketing research team, was **designed** to **gather** information about people's buying habits.

2 use appropriate nouns and noun phrases

The team interviewed a **random selection** of 100 **participants** over a four-week period.

3 use appropriate adjectives and adverbs to give a more accurate description

Prior to the study, the consultants had predicted that there would be **considerable** variation in the subjects' approach to purchasing.
They found that men spent **significantly** more time than women researching their purchases on the internet.

4 use appropriate phrases to compare data

However, women shopped **more frequently** and spent **larger sums of money** overall.

▶ See **16** *Comparing and contrasting* and **17** *Describing similarities and differences*.

---

5 use correct prepositions with nouns, verbs and adjectives

These findings are **consistent with** those of other similar studies.

▶ See **51** and **52** *Using prepositions*.

> **📋 Remember!**
>
> Write numbers from one to ten in words (eight) and numbers above ten in numerals (88). Percent can be written as one or two words (per cent).

- Here are some more examples of vocabulary commonly used to describe data:

   The experiment was **set up** in a secure environment.

   The **main aim** of the study was to **investigate** buying habits.

   The study **focused on** people aged 20–30.

   A range of **variables** had to be considered.

   The researchers were looking for **evidence** to prove their **theory**.

   Spending **varied** each day but sometimes **reached** very high **levels**.

   Woman purchased **a greater number** of items than men.

   A number of **significant differences** were found.

   The **researchers** made some interesting **observations**.

   The findings **suggest / indicate / show** that….

   Results have **revealed** a number of **significant differences**.

   Certain **conclusions** can be **drawn** from the **figures**.

   Other findings were **inconclusive**.

> **❗ Danger Zone**
>
> **Number and amount**
>
> 'Number' is usually used with countable nouns that have a plural form, such as *man/men*; and *item/items*.
>
> 'Amount' is usually used with uncountable nouns that have only one form, such as *money* and *time*.
>
> a significant amount of people ✘
> a significant number of people ✔
> the number of researches ✘
> the amount of research ✔

Exercises

1 Choose the most appropriate option in italics.

1 Trials were *conducted / designed* over a two-week period.
2 The data was carefully *explored / analysed*.
3 A number of *variables / differences* between the groups were evident.
4 The data revealed some *significant / large* differences.
5 The researchers' *thoughts / expectations* were confirmed.
6 Purchasing patterns were *consistent / the same* across the age groups.
7 See Appendix A for a summary of the *finding / findings*.
8 Consumerism has *gained / reached* an all-time high in some cities.

2 Correct the sentences.

1 At the weekend, spending rose by 8 per cent.
2 The study produced a large number of data.
3 Exactly two hundred and fifty people were interviewed.
4 The amount of volunteers surprised the research team.

3 Complete each gap with an appropriate word from the box.

results	participants	finding	aim	conducted	observations	difference	predicted	variation

A hundred (1) .... were involved in a study designed and (2) .... by a group of Head Teachers. The (3) .... of the study was to compare the reading ability of students across the secondary-school years. The teachers (4) .... that the study would show a considerable (5) .... between boys' and girls' reading scores in Years seven to nine. After that they expected less (6) ....

Their (7) .... were inconclusive. However, during the course of the study, they made a number of interesting (8) .... One of these suggests that schools would do well to encourage boys to read newspapers, rather than books – a (9) .... they intend to research further.

46 Paraphrasing

Paraphrasing is when you rewrite someone else's words using your own words.

> **Writing Tip**
>
> A good paraphrase:
> - is a useful alternative to a direct quotation
> - shows that you understand the original text
> - is normally the same length as the original text
> - always acknowledges the source.

> **Remember!**
>
> You don't need to change:
> - very common words that have no alternatives, e.g. 'television' or 'university'
> - specialised words from particular subject areas, e.g. 'limited company' or 'diagnosis'.

- Here are some extracts on the subject of charities and some techniques to combine when paraphrasing:

Using synonyms (words that mean the same)

▶ **Look at this source text and think about which words could be replaced by synonyms.**

| Companies that show a genuine interest in charitable activities can earn the respect of the buying public (Soller, 2010). |

- Here is a version of the source text, using synonyms:

Businesses that **demonstrate** a **real** interest in **non-profit-making** activities can **gain** the respect of **consumers**.

NOTE: An ordinary dictionary, a dictionary of synonyms, or a thesaurus will help you find synonyms.

Changing the form of words

▶ **Look at this source text and think about how the form of the underlined words could be changed.**

| Some charities owe their <u>success</u> to the <u>selective</u> use of consultants (Michaels, 2009). |

- Here is a version of the source text, changing the noun 'success' into the adjective 'successful', and the adjective 'selective' into the adverb 'selectively'.

Michaels (2009) states that some charities are **successful** because they use consultants **selectively**.

Changing the grammatical structure

▶ **Look at this source text and think about how a different comparative structure could be used to paraphrase the underlined part of the sentence.**

| Persuading the public to sign up to monthly donations is a <u>more cost-effective policy than</u> collecting single contributions (Polson, 2009). |

- Here is a version of the source text, using a different grammatical structure:

Collecting single contributions is **not as cost-effective as** persuading the public to sign up to monthly donations, according to Polson (2009).

- Other grammatical changes when paraphrasing could include:

active ↔ passive
The Government offered charities a tax break → Charities were offered a tax break.

despite ↔ although
Despite offering charities a tax break, the Government... → Although the Government had offered...

cause ↔ effect
Tax breaks led to increased revenue. → Charities increased their revenue because of tax breaks.

---

modal verb ↔ adjective

Charities can increase their revenue... → It is possible for charities to increase their revenue....

verb ↔ participle

Before they introduced the tax breaks, the Government → Before introducing the tax breaks...

Using all three approaches

▶ **Look at this source text. Think about how it could be paraphrased using synonyms, changing the form of words and changing a grammatical structure.**

> Indirect delivery via institutions such as the World Bank may mean that UK charity contributions are lost to corrupt practices (Gates, 2008).

- Here are some changes that can be made:
  - start with the **effect** (funds disappearing) rather than the cause
  - change the **word forms** (e.g. corrupt practices → corruption)
  - use **synonyms** (e.g. via → through; institutions → organisations)
  - change a **grammatical structure** (e.g. are lost → could disappear)

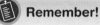 **Remember!**

You need to use more than one of these techniques to produce a full paraphrase.

- Here is a paraphrase of the source text, with the above changes:

Gates (2008) argues that British aid funds could disappear through corruption if they are distributed indirectly through organisations such as the World Bank.

❶ Danger Zone

Not mentioning your source

When you have paraphrased someone else's words, you should mention the source:

It is only in recent years that charities have begun to organise themselves along the lines of commercial businesses.
How do you know this? Where did you get this idea from? Is this your own belief or have you read it in a source?
Coleman (2009) argues that it is only in recent years that charities have begun to organise themselves along the lines of commercial businesses. ✔

Mentioning the source also gives your paraphrase more weight.　　▸ See **44** *Citing.*

Exercises

1 Replace the underlined words with synonyms.

1 Aid workers <u>need</u> *to* have a degree of <u>tolerance</u> towards cultural differences.
2 Human rights charities <u>censured</u> the <u>harsh</u> treatment of prisoners by the regime.
3 <u>Laws</u> to <u>prevent</u> bogus charities from operating were <u>wholeheartedly</u> welcomed.
4 The two charities worked <u>tirelessly</u> against the <u>damaging</u> effects of child labour.

2 Rewrite these sentences following the instructions in brackets.

1 The report advised the charity to extend the range of its projects. (use *extensive*)
2 An excess of disaster campaigns can lead to 'compassion fatigue'. (start with *Compassion fatigue...*)
3 Familiarity with local customs is essential for aid workers. (use *familiar*)
4 Although it raised enough money, FoodAid could not get supplies to the region. (use *despite* and *unable*)
5 Aid workers on the ground may need to make creative responses to unexpected situations. (use *creatively*)

3 Write paraphrases of these texts.

1 A successful aid advertisement needs to combine the elicitation of compassion with serious factual information about the state of play on the ground (Myers, 2009).
2 It is likely that the Government will ring fence its expenditure on foreign aid, whatever the pressure of its deficit-cutting programme (Davis, 2010).
3 Competition amongst charities has never been greater than it is at the moment (Briggs, 2011).

47 Formal language 1

Doctors use electrocardiograms <u>and that sort of thing</u> to investigate heart problems.	→	Doctors use **tests such as** electrocardiograms to investigate heart problems.

> 💡 **Writing Tip**
>
> The kind of language you might use in conversation is often inappropriate in academic work because it is too informal or imprecise. In your written work, you need to develop a precise, objective style and avoid colloquial language, such as slang and clichés.

Words and phrases to avoid

▶ **Read the following sentences and think about which words you would avoid in formal writing, and how you might replace them.**

1 It would be dead easy for the Government to make unhealthy foods much more expensive. ✖
2 There are loads of examples of advertising campaigns that have changed public attitudes to aspects of health. ✖
3 Gone are the days when the public would automatically pay attention to a ministerial announcement broadcast on the BBC. ✖
4 The town centre workshops were brilliant. ✖

• Here are the sentences as you might write them in an academic essay.

1 What's wrong: Colloquial language or slang terms such as *dead easy, cool, cute, kids, guys, ad, uni, skive, kip* and *doss* should be avoided in formal writing.
→ It would be **relatively straightforward** for the Government to make unhealthy foods much more expensive. ✔

2 What's wrong: Imprecise conversational language such as *loads of, a bit, a couple of, a lot of, sort of,* and *stuff* should also be avoided.
→ There are **many** examples of advertising campaigns that have changed public attitudes to aspects of health. ✔

3 What's wrong: *Gone are the days when; in a nutshell; to turn a blind eye; crystal clear; at the end of the day; to stick out like a sore thumb*: these are all examples of the clichés used in spoken English, when people have very little time to think.
→ **The era has passed when** the public would automatically pay attention to a ministerial broadcast on the BBC. ✔

4 What's wrong: Subjective expressions such as *brilliant, really good, marvellous, appalling, disgusting,* and *really bad* should be replaced with more objective or restrained terms.
→ The town centre workshops were **highly effective.** ✔

Using *it...* and *there ...*

• Starting sentences with *It ...* or *there....* rather than *I/We ...* gives your writing a more objective tone.

• In the structure **It + be/modal verb**, you can use 'it' as an impersonal subject for your sentence:

I believe that local authorities should offer more incentives to those who might be considering cycling to work.	→	**It could be argued** that local authorities should offer more incentives to those ...

• In the structure **There + be/modal verb**, you can use *there* to introduce your idea:

We can all understand why people enjoy driving their own cars.	→	**There are a number of reasons** why people enjoy driving their own cars.

- Here are some more examples:

  It seems clear that the public now recognises the link between exercise and health.

  There can be little doubt that children are influenced by what they see on television.

Remember!

Contractions such as *didn't, won't, they'll* etc. should be avoided in formal written English.

When to use *I* and *we*

'I' and 'we' are often avoided in academic English by using impersonal structures such as *It ...* and *there ...* above. There are times, however, when it can be appropriate to use these pronouns in formal writing.

Remember!

You can use words such as *essay, evidence, research, statistics* as the subjects of your sentences to give a more impersonal tone, e.g. This essay will discuss...; Research has shown that ...; Statistics suggest that ...

- 'I' (or 'we' if you are working in a group) can be used when you are describing the scope of your argument:

  In the conclusion, **I** will make some recommendations for encouraging children to eat in a more healthy way.

  ▶ See **49** *The language of argument.*

- 'I' (often with *would*) can be used to clarify your position during an essay. Useful verbs include *accept, argue, consider, propose, suggest*:

  I would accept, however, that this argument has not yet been won.

- 'We' can be used when you see yourself as part of a group or community:

  Unless **we** take positive action, children who are growing up today will face the avoidable medical conditions that result from overeating.

  (*we* = society)

Exercises

1 Amend the sentences, to avoid colloquial or slang terms.

  1 One ad in a successful campaign shows a young dad in a park, looking after a couple of kids, and failing to notice some of the dangers present in the situation.
  2 In the promotion of their food products, some companies turn a blind eye to the health risks posed to young children.
  3 Encouraging young people in the notion that it is cool to become drunk is disgusting.
  4 If young people suspect that they are to become the subject of a lecture, they may avoid the campaign message like the plague.
  5 Ronson points out that sedentary lifestyles can be found as often amongst the pen pushers at the office as within the home.
  6 The problem of overeating won't be sorted by health campaigns on their own.

2 Rewrite these sentences, using *it* or *there* rather than *I* or *we*.

  1 I think that food and drink advertisements that target children under ten should be banned.
  2 We have to recognise that cars play an important role in a person's sense of autonomy.
  3 I believe in the food industry regulating itself in the area of advertising, rather than in creating new laws.
  4 We have seen a greater demand amongst consumers for information about the food and drink that they purchase.
  5 We must not forget that the costs of treating the illnesses brought about by unhealthy lifestyles are shared by the whole of society.
  6 I am convinced that young people are now much more aware of the dangers of alcohol abuse.

48   Formal language 2

Formal grammar

Formal written language is tighter and often briefer than conversational language. A number of key grammatical features contribute to making formal, written language different from the 'looser', spoken form.

- The use of **relative clauses** to convey additional information:

The Democratic Republic of the Congo is Africa's second largest country. It used to be a Belgian colony.	The Democratic Republic of the Congo, **which used to be a Belgian colony**, is Africa's second largest country.

  ◆ See **15** *Relative clauses.*

- Building sentences around **nouns** rather than verbs or adjectives:

It is easy to understand why the country objected at first to having peacekeeping forces within its borders.	The country's initial **objection** to peacekeeping forces within its borders is understandable.

  ◆ See **18** *Using noun phrases.*

- Using **the passive** for a style that focuses on an event rather than a person or people:

Officials set up polling stations in every community across the region.	Polling stations **were set up** in every community across the region.

  ◆ See **7** *Using the passive.*

- Using **a single complex word** instead of a phrase:

People began to lose their faith in the new Government when it stopped people from leaving their houses after dusk.	**Disillusionment** with the new Government set in when a dusk **curfew** was imposed.

  ◆ See **53** *Using longer words* and **54** *Using single words for impact.*

- Using **sophisticated** rather than simple **linkers**:

The situation continued to be unstable, but people queued all day at the polling stations.	**Despite** the instability of the situation, people queued all day at the polling stations.

  ◆ See **26–29** *Linking.*

- Using words and techniques to make **different parts** of your writing **fit together** in a more formal way:

Kasa-Vubu, who was President of the Congo, and Lumumba, who was the Prime Minister, adopted significantly different approaches to the country's relationship with Belgium.	Kasa-Vubu and Lumumba, President and Prime Minister of the Congo **respectively**, adopted significantly different approaches to the country's relationship with Belgium.

  ◆ See **30** *Signposting,* **31** *Using pronouns correctly* and **32** *Avoiding repetition of words.*

📋 Remember!

No, little and *few* sound more formal than *not any, not much,* and *not many* respectively:
There are **no** easy answers. There is **little** that can be done. There are **few** obvious remedies.

Formal vocabulary

▶ **Some words and phrases have more formal, sometimes Latin-based equivalents.**

● Read the following sentences and think about how the underlined words might be replaced in formal writing:
The situation <u>got worse</u>, however, after the elections.
Errors in the electoral process were described by the regime as <u>very small</u>.
For many citizens <u>the existing situation</u> was no longer acceptable.

● Here are the sentences as you might write them in an academic essay.

The situation **deteriorated**, however, after the elections.

Other verbs with more formal equivalents include: deal with (e.g. a problem) → **address**; get → **acquire/obtain**; give (to charity) → **donate**; help → **assist**; show → **demonstrate**.

♦ See also **55** *Phrasal verbs*.

Errors in the electoral process were described by the regime as **negligible**.

Other adjectives with more formal equivalents include: very bad → **unacceptable**; big/large → **substantial**; difficult → **problematic**; fair → **justifiable**; very powerful → **overwhelming**.

For many citizens **the status quo** was no longer acceptable.

This is an example of a Latin phrase commonly used in academic writing. Others include:

bona fide (genuine): Voters doubted that the building was a **bona fide** polling station.
de facto (existing, but not officially agreed): It may be necessary to negotiate with a **de facto** government, until an internationally accepted administration is established.
per capita (per head/for each person): The **per capita** annual income in the region is estimated to be $300.
pro rata (in proportion): By inviting opposition politicians into his Cabinet, the Prime Minister accepted a **pro rata** loss in his party's overall power.
vice versa (reversing the order of two things just mentioned): The economic situation often determines political decisions rather than **vice versa**.

Remember!
Some tutors may prefer you not to use Latin terms. Check whether your department has a policy on their use.

Exercises

1 Rewrite the sentences, following the instructions in brackets.

1 An enquiry has been initiated into voting irregularities. The irregularities seemed to have occurred in the north of the region. (*Combine the sentences using 'that'.*)
2 The President spoke briefly with the leader of the majority party, before the leader was pronounced Prime Minister. (*Use the words 'consultation' and 'latter'.*)
3 The governing party enacted a series of laws to grant religious freedom to the population. (Start with *A series ...* and leave out *the governing party.*)
4 Monitors had to ensure that all the adults in the region could get to polling stations. (Use *accessible.*)

2 Replace the underlined text with a more formal word or Latin phrase.

1 The Prime Minister successfully <u>dealt with</u> the major problems facing the country's infrastructure.
2 The rebel forces were defeated by the the army's <u>very powerful</u> weaponry.
3 An <u>unofficial</u> leader has emerged from the ranks of the rebel army.
4 Steyn argues that in the process of nation building, capitalism promotes political freedom and <u>the same applies the other way round</u>.
5 A lack of electricity means that factory workers can only be employed for half the day, resulting in a <u>proportionate</u> reduction in their wages.

49 The language of argument

<table>
<tr><td>To what extent has the fair trade movement been a success?</td><td>→</td><td>In order to address this question successfully, you need to use an acceptable, academic style of language.</td></tr>
</table>

🔆 Writing Tip

When you are planning your next assignment, highlight some of the words and phrases in this unit that you could use.

- Here are some examples of the language you can use for each part of an essay.

Stating the scope

▶ **Read this introduction to an essay on 'fair trade' and think about the function of the words in bold.**

First, this essay will **define** the term 'fair trade' and **describe** in brief the history of the movement. **Then** it will **consider** three cases where fair trade initiatives have benefited communities in the developing world, and **examine** with statistical evidence how general these benefits have been. **Next**, it will **move on to** criticisms of the movement, **analysing** two important concerns that have been raised in the last five years. It will **conclude** by making a recommendation for the future of the scheme.

- Stating the scope of your essay normally involves verbs such as: analyse, consider, define, examine and sequencing language such as: first, in the second part/half, next, then, finally; start, move on to, follow, finish, conclude

Your thesis statement

- Your department may require a 'thesis statement', summarising your point of view in one sentence near the beginning of your essay. Thesis statements often use the modal verbs should, will, can, ought to and sometimes connectors, such as however, although, despite/in spite of.

I will argue that the fair trade movement, **despite** some of its failures, **should** be supported and improved.

Supporting your claims

- You should make clear that claims and views you express are supported by concrete evidence, and not simply personal opinions that you cannot back up. The introductory phrases below are therefore more appropriate than expressions such as 'I think', 'the way I see it', 'I do not agree':

  It can be argued that …
  (On balance), it seems that …
  One of the main arguments for X is that …
  The first point to be made is that …

- To support your views, you can refer to research:

  Statistics indicate that …
  Research demonstrates that …
  Studies have shown that …

  ▶ See **44** *Citing* and **46** *Paraphrasing*.

- You can also provide examples to illustrate your arguments:

  Take for example, to illustrate, such as

  ▶ See **43** *Introducing an example.*

- You can link your supporting claims by using: secondly, thirdly, finally and connectors such as: furthermore, as well as, in addition to

  ▶ See **27** *Linking: adding.*

📋 Remember!

If there is evidence to support your view, you should refer to it. Otherwise your view will lose impact or raise unanswered questions in the reader's mind.

Commenting on counter-arguments

● To provide a balanced viewpoint, you may wish to comment on opposing arguments.

> **Despite** these successes, there is an argument that very little financial benefit actually reaches farmers in the producer countries (Griffiths 2010). This is a claim which it is difficult to prove, **however**, as there has been so little formal research into the impact of fair trade measures in developing countries.

● You can signal this by using connectors that express contrast such as: although, but, despite, however, while
  ◗ See **26** *Linking: contrasting.*
● You can introduce other counter-arguments with the structure:
  Another/a second etc./a further argument against fair trade is that ...
  Another/a second etc./a further objection to fair trade is that ...

Drawing conclusions and making recommendations

● To introduce a conclusion, you can use a fixed expression such as:

To conclude, ...	In conclusion, ...	To sum up, ...	Clearly, therefore, ...
To summarise, ...	In summary, ...	As we have seen, ...	On balance, ...

  or you can begin a clause:
  We can say that .../It can be said that ...
  Thus, we can conclude that .../it can be concluded that ...
  On the basis of these arguments, we can conclude that .../it can be concluded that ...
● To make a recommendation, you can use an introductory phrase such as:
  On the basis of these arguments, it would be advisable (for someone/something) to + verb ...
  It follows that there is a (pressing/urgent) need (for someone/something) to + verb ...
  or you can use a sentence ending in the passive form:
  ... should/must be done/carried out.
  ... is (therefore) recommended/needed.
  ... could/should be considered.

> **To conclude**, given that more than forty years have passed since the slogan 'Trade not aid' was adopted at the United Nations Conference on Trade and Development, **it seems clear that** an independent formal impact study with access to all the relevant data **should be carried out**.

Exercises

1 **You are answering the question 'Globalisation has as many casualties as success stories.' Use the essay outline below to state the scope of your essay.**
  1 Definition of globalisation
  2 Drawbacks of globalisation in developing countries
  3 Loss of cultural identity
  4 Political gains
  5 Success in international campaigns
  6 Conclusion: benefits outweigh disadvantages

2 **Correct these sentences by amending or changing one word in each.**
  1 It can be argue that economic globalisation has produced a 'sweatshop' working culture in some regions.
  2 A further objection for economic globalisation comes from fair trade theorists who argue that unrestricted free trade will always benefit richer nations.
  3 The first point to be making is that some cultural changes operate at a very superficial level.
  4 Despite some aspects of political change have been accelerated by globalisation, other regional factors also need to be taken into account.
  5 Studies have show that views on globalisation have become more polarised in the last ten years.
  6 It follows that it is a pressing need for an international agreement on basic minimum working conditions in the clothing industry.

50   Adjectives & adverbs

An **adjective** goes with a **noun**

rapid + change

A **verb** goes with an **adverb**

changed + rapidly

Some **adverbs** can go with an **adjective** or another **adverb**

extremely + rapid   extremely + rapidly

💡 **Writing Tip**

Using adjectives and adverbs correctly can greatly improve your writing, particularly if you use ones that convey your meaning precisely.

▶ **Read this paragraph from an essay about changes in the music industry, look at the adverbs (in bold), then read the rules.**

The music industry has **frequently** undergone major changes and it has always tried **hard** to adapt. It has been affected **equally** by technological advances and demographic changes in its market. A structure that worked **well** in one decade would prove not to be viable in another. For example, the domination of big record companies came to an end **remarkably quickly** in the 1990s. Small independent companies could now produce and market music **easily** and set-up costs for such companies were **reasonably** low. **Logically**, this had major repercussions for the big companies.

⋔ Rules

Forming adverbs

Most adverbs are formed by adding **-ly** to the adjective:

clear → clearly   extreme → extremely

If the adjective ends with -l, add **-ly**:

full → fully   essential → essentially
global → globally

If the adjective ends with -y, the adverb ends with **-ily**:

happy → happily

If the adjective ends with **-ble**, the adverb ends with **-bly**:

considerable → considerably   incredible → incredibly

If the adjective ends with **-ic**, the adverb ends **-ically**:

basic → basically

The adverb form of **good** is **well**:

a good idea → an idea that works well

For these common words, the adverb is the same as the adjective:

fast → fast   hard → hard   late → late

- It is often possible to say the same thing using an adjective or an adverb:
  He felt under **constant pressure**. / He felt **constantly under pressure**.
  The adjective 'constant' describes the noun' pressure; the adverb 'constantly' goes with the verb 'felt'.

- You can vary the position of an adverb depending on what you want to emphasise:
  He felt **constantly** under pressure. OR He felt under pressure **constantly**.

📋 Remember!

- Never use the adverb 'well' with the meaning 'very' in academic writing.
  Initially, the music industry was well pleased with its response to the challenge. ❌

- Use more sophisticated adverbs instead of 'very' 'really' or 'a lot' in order to give your work a more academic style:
  It proved ~~very~~ **extraordinarily** difficult for them to adapt to new technologies.
  At that time, record companies were ~~really~~ **remarkably** quick to adapt to changing fashions.
  Soon, the whole picture had changed ~~a lot~~ **considerably**.

Adverbs for commenting

- Adverbs are used in academic writing to comment on a situation or fact. They can carry quite complex ideas in a very brief way, and this makes them a useful tool in academic writing.
- Here are some examples:

  1 A personal comment:

  Admittedly, some electronic music has been outstanding in terms of composition. (I admit that…)

  2 A general comment:

  Clearly, solutions need to be found a soon as possible. (It is clear that…)

  The effects of this development on the music industry were, **unsurprisingly**, enormous. (There was no surprise about this.)

  3 A suggestion that something may not be true:

  Apparently, this problem was insurmountable for the producers.

  There were, **allegedly**, a number of sharp practices in the industry at that time.

  Seemingly, no-one knew about the problem at the time.

  (This is what has been said but it seems hard to believe.)

NOTE: An adverb can begin a sentence, in which case it should be followed by a comma, or come between commas later in a sentence.

ⓘ Danger Zone

Using an adjective when an adverb is required

An adverb 'describes 'a verb – it gives information on how something is done or happens, or it describes an action. Most adverbs end -ly. Don't use an adjective when an adverb is required.

The situation improved tremendous and profits rose steady. ✖

The situation **improved tremendously** and profits rose **steadily**. ✔

Exercises

1 Find the five incorrectly spelt adverbs in this paragraph and correct them.

This was definitly the beginning of a new era. Specially formed labels within the major record companies, catering for niche markets that were continualy appearing, became the norm. People who enthusiastically followed styles of music that had previously been very much minority interests now found that the records they wanted to buy were readyly available in shops. Inevitabley, there were parallel developments in radio. Shows catering exclusively for these individual styles of music suddenly sprang up, and these rapidly acquired dedicated listeners, who immediatly went out and bought the records they heard on the shows.

2 Decide if the underlined adjectives and adverbs are correct or not and correct those that are not.

1 This was a problem that proved <u>incredible</u> difficult to solve.
2 There are many other people who behave <u>similar</u> in these circumstances.
3 The idea became <u>extraordinarily</u> popular within a short space of time.
4 Attitudes to this issue have undergone <u>drastic</u> changes in recent years.
5 People made a <u>desperately</u> attempt to avoid the oncoming disaster.
6 People in the audience were <u>well</u> impressed by the performance.

3 Rewrite these sentences, replacing the underlined phrases with an adverb.

1 <u>It was astonishing that</u> nobody had noticed this problem before.
2 Similar research was going on elsewhere, <u>which was a coincidence</u>.
3 <u>It was unfortunate</u> that nobody foresaw this problem.
4 <u>It is obvious that</u> no firm conclusions can be drawn from such little evidence.
5 Nothing could have been done to prevent the accident, <u>it appears</u>.

51   Using prepositions 1

Prepositions complete phrases or form a relationship between words in a sentence.
Common prepositions include: at, of, in, on, for, off, out of, from, by, with, without.
Other prepositions include: as, beyond, against, throughout, between, concerning, towards.

> 💡 **Writing Tip**
>
> Prepositions are widely used in English but, unfortunately, there are few rules for their use. Good writers learn combinations of words and prepositions that are relevant to their subjects.

▶ **Here are some features of prepositions:**

- They have a meaning of their own and can be used to indicate time, movement, place, etc. in both concrete and abstract ways:
  over the wall; **over** a ten-year period / **towards** the goal; **towards** success / **beyond** our galaxy; **beyond** anyone's dreams
- They can go with many verbs, adjectives and nouns:
  believe **in** / different **from** / characteristics **of**
- They can form part of a common phrase:
  to what extent / **in** contrast **to** / **in** line **with** / **on** account **of**
- They can form part of a phrasal verb:
  carry **out** / draw **on** / weigh **up** / account **for**
  ▸ See **55** *Phrasal verbs.*

Prepositions with verbs, adjectives and nouns

▶ **Here are some examples that you might need to use in academic work:**

1 **to report information (verbs)**
   White (2008) points out, admits to, agrees to / agrees with X on / about something, reflects on, accuses X of, refers to, expresses doubts / concerns about / over, draws attention to, focuses on, gives / lends support to
2 **to introduce or describe research/a study, etc.**
   conduct research into, be involved in, do a study on, be based on, focus / centre on, the aim / focus of, find out about, an analysis of, provide evidence of / for, present findings / a paper on
3 **to describe and compare data/results, etc.**
   rise / increase to (a figure), align with, a rise / increase / difference of (a figure), correspond to, a rise / increase / difference in something, similar to / different from, stabilise at, equivalent to, fluctuate between, be consistent with, peak at / (a) peak of, correlation between, compare / contrast with, a proportion of, an overview of
4 **to discuss advantages and disadvantages**
   an advantage / disadvantage / of / of -ing, an advantage / disadvantage / benefit / drawback for someone, benefit from, be of benefit to
5 **to define**
   define / name as, unique to, a description of, refer to X as, specific to, an / place emphasis on, classify into (groups), inherent in, knowledge about / of, distinguish between, a definition of, an image / picture of
6 **to describe cause and effect relationships**
   result in, a relationship with, dependent on, a repercussion of, a consequence / outcome of, implications of, an impact / effect / influence on / of X, a factor in
7 **to give reasons and explanations**
   account for, an indication / indicative of, an example of, contribute to, point to / towards, a reason / explanation for, lie beneath, a justification for

▶ Here are some additional points about prepositions and verbs:

- If a verb follows a preposition, the verb must be in the 'ing' form:
  Despite evidence to the contrary, Mackie (2003) insisted on argue that he was right. ✗
  Despite evidence to the contrary, Mackie (2003) **insisted on arguing** that he was right. ✓
- It is often better to put the preposition before a relative pronoun in formal English:
  This is the research that Cairns based her theory of molecular attraction on. ✗
  This is the research **on which** Cairns based her theory of molecular attraction. ✓
  Peterson was the politician that most people in rural areas voted for. ✗
  Peterson was the politician **for whom** most people in rural areas voted. ✓
  ▸ See 'Prepositions in relative clauses' in **15**.

> **!** **Danger Zone**
>
> **Omitting 'the fact (that)'**
>
> A preposition cannot be followed by 'that' if it is being used as a linking word.
> No one was aware of that they were being filmed. ✗
> There was some discussion about that some of the results looked misleading. ✗
> - Sometimes the preposition can simply be dropped.
>   No one was aware that they were being filmed. ✓
> - At other times, 'the fact' must be added before 'that':
>   No one was **aware of the fact that** they were being filmed. ✓
>   There was some **discussion about the fact that** some of the results looked misleading. ✓

Exercises

1 Complete each gap with the correct preposition.

1 The reviewers expressed some doubts .... the authenticity of the material and, as a result, the writer was accused .... plagiarism.
2 When the results of the survey were analysed, it was observed that there had been an increase ....
   5 percent ..... reading scores, which was consistent ..... previous years.
3 The field trip, conducted by a group of geologists, was designed to provide the department ...... a better overview ...... the surrounding area.
4 Some problems, inherent ...... the nature of research and its narrow focus ..... particular subjects or sub-groups, cannot be readily avoided.
5 In order to account ...... the discrepancies in their data, the research team drew their critics' attention ...... some of the experimental constraints.

2 Decide whether the sentences are correct or not. Correct the sentences that are incorrect.

1 Everything seemed to point to that they were going to lose their funding.
2 The use of a placebo is a method specific to clinical trials.
3 The department had to deal with the repercussions of they assigned difficult projects to junior staff.
4 Having presented the findings, the group then compared them with similar outcomes from other studies.

3 Rewrite the sentences so that the preposition does not come at the end.

1 This is the area that we have most knowledge about.
2 Here are the results that I based my assessment on.
3 The survey identified individuals that there is no current provision for.
4 You need to look at the groups the insects have been classified into.
5 Sometimes there are problems that we do not have explanations for.
6 It turned out to be a situation that most people benefited from.

52 Using prepositions 2

A **correct preposition** clarifies meaning; an **incorrect** or **unnecessary** one obscures it.

You must comply ~~to~~ **with** the confidentiality agreement.
We will explore ~~on~~ this topic in the next session.

> 💡 **Writing Tip**
>
> It is essential to know which prepositions to use with certain words and which prepositions are used in certain phrases.

▶ **Here are some reasons why mistakes are made using prepositions:**

1 Sometimes different prepositions can be used with the same word:
Meals were **provided for** the participants during the study. (*for + somebody*)
The results **provided** the researchers **with** the information that they needed. (*with + something*)
- The correct choice depends on what the preposition is followed by.

2 Sometimes the word is not followed by a preposition at all:
The article highlighted ~~on~~ the main ideas of Peterson.
You might make this type of mistake because:
- a synonym of the word goes with the preposition:

  | highlight ~~on~~ | → | focus **on** | enhance ~~on~~ | → | improve **on** |
  | relish ~~in~~ | → | delight **in** | comprise ~~of~~ | → | consist **of** |

- The meaning of the sentence (wrongly) suggests the preposition is needed:

  enhance ~~to~~   →   'to' carries the idea of adding something
  eliminate ~~out~~   →   'out' carries the idea of something being removed

- The base word or another form of the word can be used with the preposition:

  enforce ~~to~~   →   to force someone **to**

- A related phrase goes with the preposition:

  to research ~~on~~   →   to do research **on**
  to emphasise ~~on~~   →   to place emphasis **on**
  to discuss ~~about~~   →   to have a discussion **about**

- The verb can be used with and without the preposition depending on the context and meaning:
  Peterson **found** ~~out~~ several anomalies in his data.
  Peterson **found out** why his data was corrupt.

3 Sometimes an object comes between a verb and its preposition:
We have **devoted** all our time **to** this question.
- The further away the preposition is from the verb, the greater the possibility for error.
  The noise **distracted** <u>everyone in the lecture hall</u> ~~on~~ **from** the task.

Prepositional phrases

▶ **Phrases that start with prepositions can cause problems for students. Here are some examples of correct use:**

in someone's view / from someone's point of view / in the view of
- These are all ways of expressing people's opinions.
  In Lyle's view, there is little support for such a theory.
  From Lyle's point of view, there is little support for such a theory.
  In the view of some technicians, safety in the laboratory could be improved.

> 📋 **Remember!**
>
> Some common phrases are widely misused, but this does not make them correct:
>
> There is no point ~~of~~ **in** doing research on a very small sample.
>
> All the statistics supported the theory except ~~from~~ **for** the final batch.
>
> Learn the correct prepositions in these cases and this will help your writing improve.

in view of / with a view to

- The first phrase means 'because of'; the second means 'with the aim of'.

  In view of the safety issues, the laboratory has been temporarily closed.

  Work is being undertaken, **with a view to** re-opening the laboratory in the next few days.

with the exception of / except for

- Both phrases mean 'apart from'; the first is more formal.

  All the experiments took place on the campus **with the exception of** the control test.

  All the experiments took place on the campus **except for** the control test.

in line with / in keeping with

- These phrases mean 'consistent with' or 'in the same style as'.

  The arguments put forward by Browne are **in line with** current thinking.

  It is important for the tone of a piece of writing to be **in keeping with** its general purpose.

with regard to / in terms of

- The first phrase means 'in connection with'; the second clarifies the particular issue you wish to discuss.

  A great deal of discussion took place **with regard to** the outcome of the trial.

  The trial was well run **in terms of** its timing but other aspects could have been better organised.

in respect of / in connection with

- Both phrases mean 'on the subject of' or 'regarding'.

  I am writing **in respect of** / **in connection with** my recent application.

on account of / in the light of

- Both phrases introduce a reason or explanation.

  In the light of increasing student numbers, more research staff have been taken on.

  No work will be done on the project **on account of** the staff shortage.

on reflection / in retrospect / with hindsight

- The first phrase means 'thinking about it'; the second and third mean 'looking back'.

  On reflection, it would have been better to use a different method of analysis.

  The emphasis placed on external influences was, **in retrospect/in hindsight**, too great.

Exercises

1 Choose the correct alternative to complete the sentences.

1 The researchers *found / found out* some anomalies in their data.
2 Some people have devoted their lives *to/in* the pursuit of knowledge.
3 Everyone *except from/apart from* Goh has supported this theory.
4 I have decided to *research/research on* a different area.
5 The equipment *comprises of/consists of* a bell jar, a funnel and a tube.
6 There is no point *of/in* presenting a claim if you cannot back it up.

2 Complete the gaps in the sentences with the correct noun.

1 No differences were found with .... to drug tolerance levels.
2 All layout and design features must be in ..... with standard practice.
3 In Graham's ...., more research is needed before any definitive conclusions can be drawn.
4 On ...... of the huge turnout, the lecture room was changed at the last minute.
5 In ...., better results might have been achieved if the final phase had been less rushed.
6 Nothing has been agreed in ..... of future research plans.
7 All analyses in this investigation, with the .... of one, were completed on time.
8 Certain activities have been cut from the budget in the .... of the economic downturn.

3 Rewrite these sentences using the words in brackets and starting with the underlined words.

1 These are the aspects <u>I would</u> like to emphasise. (place emphasis)
2 Because of the changes in the schedule, <u>a postponement</u> is in order. (view)
3 <u>We need</u> to discuss some of the conclusions. (discussion about)
4 The sombre background made <u>certain features</u> stand out. (highlighted)

53 Using longer words

At its worst, according to Stern (2008), business forecasting is a science <u>that cannot be relied upon</u>, hiding itself in <u>language that we cannot comprehend</u>.

→

At its worst, according to Stern (2008), business forecasting is an **unreliable** science, hiding itself in **incomprehensible** language.

> 💡 **Writing Tip**
>
> Forming longer, more complex words will improve the style of your work and create a better impression than using simple, common or short words.

Forming longer words

This often involves adding a prefix and/or suffix to a word to create a longer and more complex word:

think → unthinkable   appear → disappearance   theory → theoretically

- **Prefixes**, such as *in, ir, dis, un, non*, etc., are added to the beginning of words. They often give words a negative or opposite meaning; e.g. *relevant → irrelevant*.
  NOTE: some prefixes, such as *non*, are followed by a hyphen → *non-existent*.

- **Suffixes**, such as *ly, ful, wise, able, ness*, etc., are added to the ends of words to modify their meaning. They often change the part of speech and alter the spelling of the word; e.g. *regret* (noun) → *regrettable* (adjective).

Using longer words

▶ **Read this paragraph from a business case study and look at the words used to express the key ideas.**

> When consultants were called in to advise on how the organisation should **implement** change, they **recommended** several things. They **advised against** rapid change and suggested that management should **consult** staff on the subject for a fairly **long** period. They said that some of the ideas the management were **proposing** would **not work** because they were too **complex,** and they mentioned how **unpopular** the suggested productivity scheme would be. The consultants also stressed the need for management and staff to work together in **harmony**.

What's wrong: Simple words are used too often, where longer and more complex words could be formed to express the ideas in a more sophisticated and academic style.

- Here is the paragraph with better wording:

When consultants were called in to advise the organisation on the **implementation** of change, they made several **recommendations**. They said that rapid change was **inadvisable** and suggested a **lengthy** period of **consultation** between management and staff. They described some of the management's **proposals** as **unworkable** because of their **complexity** and mentioned the likely **unpopularity** of the productivity scheme. They also stressed the need for management and staff to work together **harmoniously**.

Using suffixes and prefixes to enhance vocabulary use may involve forming:

1 Nouns

Indecisiveness at senior management level and **misfortune** in terms of global market conditions proved to be a fatal **combination**.

2 Adjectives

The **innovative** approach taken to marketing was the main **contributory** factor in the **extraordinary** success of the product.

3 Adverbs

Initially, they felt that it would be best to proceed **cautiously**, and so they **temporarily** kept staffing at the lowest possible level.

4 Verbs

Rather than **endanger** the whole future of the company, the board decided to **minimise** expenditure on speculative projects and to **strengthen** its core operations.

! Danger Zone

Spelling mistakes

When you add a prefix and/or suffix to a word (affixation), the new word may have a different spelling.
e.g. *temporary* → *temporarily*   *temporaryly* ✗

Although there are some spelling rules for affixation, they are hard to remember and there are many exceptions. So it is better to learn how to spell each individual word.
The comment was *unnecessary* and *unhelpful*. ✓
unecessary ✗
unhelpfull ✗
NOTE: The suffix 'ful' does not have double 'l'.
▸ See **58** *Key spelling rules* and **59** *Common spelling mistakes*.

Exercises

1 Create the correct longer words from the words in brackets.

1   The .... (likely) of further .... (certain) in the travel sector .... (strong) the board's view that .... (expand) should be put on hold.
2   Although the aviation industry is a major (contribute) .... to the (environment) .... problems we face today, the rise in air travel seems to be (stop) ....
3   The company decided to carry out a critical (assess) .... of their business systems as many of them had become (date) .... and were causing certain sectors to (perform) ....
4   In all (probable) ...., the (technology) .... innovations taking place will bring about a (transform)......... of the industry.
5   His time as CEO of the company was (character) .... by a (disappoint) .... (imagine) .... approach to (lead) ....

2 Rewrite this paragraph, replacing the words in bold with longer words.

People **disagreed** as to which course of action would have the most **effect**. The company's founders felt with some **passion** that their position was the correct one and they had **no sympathy** with the views of others. This is an **example** of the kind of struggle going on within many organisations at the time.

3 Use a prefix to make these words mean the opposite or have a negative meaning.

1	heartening	....	7	respective	....
2	logical	....	8	orderly	....
3	justifiable	....	9	consistent	....
4	estimate	....	10	natural	....
5	conceivable	....	11	legal	....
6	compliant	....	12	pure	....

54   Using single words for impact

Using a single word for impact may involve:

1 forming a longer word using a prefix or suffix (♦ see **53** *Using longer words*)
When the councillor read the minutes of the meeting, he found that his views had <u>not been</u> **presented** <u>properly</u>.

When the councillor read the minutes of the meeting, he found that his views had been **misrepresented**.

2 using one word instead of a spoken phrase
Some members of the council had to make the same point <u>again and again</u> before it was addressed.

Some members of the council had to make the same point **repeatedly** before it was addressed.

3 using a precise word instead of a phrase (i.e. the 'right' word)
A list of items for discussion at the next meeting was prepared.

An **agenda** for the next meeting was prepared.

▶ **Read this extract from an economics essay. Think about places where a phrase could be replaced by a single, powerful word.**

People soon realised that such a high level of growth could not be sustained. Questions then arose as to what should be put first. Politicians wanted to make sure that existing standards of living were safe but many economists had a different point of view. They felt that taking only a short-term view was a mistake, even if the desire to do this was easy to understand. What could not be disputed, however, was that the country was entering a new economic phase.

What's wrong: Longer phrases are used when a single word would have more impact.

● Here is the extract with more precise wording:

It soon became apparent that such a high level of growth was **unsustainable**. Questions then arose as to what should be **prioritised**. Politicians wanted to **safeguard** existing standards of living but many economists thought **differently**. They felt that taking only a short-term view was a mistake, even if the **desirability** of doing this was **understandable**. What was **indisputable**, however, was that the country was entering a new economic phase.

● Here are some more examples:

The need for tough economic measures <u>could not be denied</u>.	→	The need for tough economic measures was **undeniable**.
When the tax rules were <u>made clearer</u>, revenues from taxation rose <u>a great deal</u>.	→	When the tax rules were **clarified**, revenues from taxation rose **considerably**.
<u>People who are against</u> the idea say that high taxation <u>causes people not to want to</u> work hard.	→	**Opponents** of the idea say that high taxation is a **disincentive** to hard work.
Some measures had effects that <u>were not foreseen</u> and caused the situation to <u>get worse</u>.	→	Some measures had **unforeseen** effects that caused the situation to **deteriorate**.

Exercises

1 **Complete the rewritten sentences, using one word instead of the underlined phrase. Form the word from one of the underlined words.**

1 <u>There can be no doubt that</u> this is one of the most urgent problems facing many governments today.
.... , this is one of the most urgent problems facing many governments today.

2 The new legislation was <u>impossible</u> for most people, even experts, <u>to comprehend</u>.
The new legislation was .... to most people, even experts.

3 The Minister felt that that the public had <u>understood</u> her words <u>in the wrong way</u>.
The Minister felt that that the public had .... her words.

4 The Foreign Office believes that if the UK can broker a peace settlement in the region, the local economic gains would be so great that they could <u>not</u> be <u>measured</u>.
The Foreign Office believes that if the UK can broker a peace settlement in the region, the local economic gains would be ....

2 **Complete the rewritten sentences, using one word instead of the underlined phrase.**

1 The results of this management theory were <u>not the same in every case</u>.
The results of this management theory were *var* ....

2 This incident <u>showed clearly</u> a major problem within the organisation.
This incident *high*............................. a major problem within the organisation.

3 Unfortunately the country lacked the <u>basic services and systems needed by the company</u>.
Unfortunately the country lacked the necessary *infra* ....

4 A problem with cash flow often leads to <u>companies going out of business</u>.
A problem with cash flow often leads to *ban*............ .

5 The pressure <u>of prices going up</u> can cause governments or central banks to increase interest rates.
Inf........... pressure can cause governments or central banks to increase interest rates.

6 Some backbench MPs argued that the proposed change was so fundamental that the public should be offered a <u>special vote on the issue</u>.
Some backbench MPs argued that the proposed change was so fundamental that the public should be offered a *ref*............................ .

3 **Rewrite the sentences using the word in brackets.**

1 It is a sector where many companies compete with each other. (competitive)
....

2 Many small businesses manage their stock-taking by computer. (computerised)
....

3 It is crucial even for a well-established company to do new things. (innovation)
....

4 Staff can lose their desire to work if managers fail to communicate. (demotivated)
....

5 People say that the company was in breach of health and safety laws. (allegedly)
....

55   Phrasal verbs

A **phrasal verb** consists of a **verb** and **one or more prepositions**.

The meaning of a phrasal verb is often different from any usual meaning of the verb or any logical meaning of the phrase.

Look at this example: Researchers **carried out** an experiment.

This phrasal verb means 'perform' or 'conduct'. It does not describe physically carrying something and it does not describe something being 'out'.

Other examples of phrasal verbs are bring about (= cause) or put up with (= tolerate).

> 💡 **Writing Tip**
>
> Many phrasal verbs are used in informal, spoken language and are not appropriate for academic writing. Others, however, are appropriate and useful in academic writing. Make sure you know which ones to use.

Informal use of phrasal verbs

▶ **Read the following paragraph from a business essay, thinking about which words or phrases should be avoided in formal writing, and how you would replace them.**

Some small companies get by for many years by putting off difficult decisions. If a business is to thrive, however, it needs to pick out its weaknesses and face up to the challenges of operating in the modern business environment. A recession, for example, may be an ideal time to check out successful competitors and come up with new business ideas. Going for that approach is better than hanging on in the hope that something turns up and tides the company over until better conditions return.

What's wrong: The over-use of phrasal verbs gives this text a rather informal tone, and some verbs (*get by, dip into, tide over, turn up*) are normally too colloquial for academic use.

- Many phrasal verbs have direct, more formal equivalents:
  get by → survive   put off → postpone   pick out → identify   face up to → confront
  check out → investigate   come up with → devise   go for → choose
- Others can be 'translated' into more formal English, sometimes by using another phrase. In the context above, you could write:
  hang on → take no action   turns up → appears by chance
  tides the company over → keeps the company solvent

▶ **Here is a rewritten version of the paragraph:**

Some small companies **survive** for many years by **postponing** difficult decisions. If a business is to thrive, however, it needs to **identify** and **confront** the challenges of operating in the modern business environment. A recession, for example, may be an ideal time to **investigate** successful competitors and **devise** new business ideas. **Choosing** that approach is better than **taking no action** in the hope that something **appears by chance** and **keeps the company solvent** until better conditions return.

Phrasal verbs in academic writing

- A number of phrasal verbs are regularly used in formal writing:

Writing about arguments

allow for (include when planning)	In her study, Professor Cresswell **allows for** the fact that members of the public sometimes exaggerate their accounts.
draw on (use resources)	Phillips **draws on** a considerable body of research to make his case.

hold up (remain strong)	Critics suggest that some of Britt's arguments do not **hold up** under scrutiny.
keep to (be relevant)	Stein has been accused of not **keeping to** the subject in his more controversial articles.
point up (emphasise)	A number of studies **point up** the importance of the research undertaken at the University of Wisconsin-Madison.
put forward (propose)	Gregory **puts forward** three key arguments in the first part of her report.
set out (present)	The case for change is clearly **set out** in the last of the team's publications.
weigh up (consider carefully)	Peterson **weighs up** both options in his paper, before making a recommendation.

Writing about public affairs

bail out (rescue financially)	Most economists agree that the Government had no choice but to **bail out** a number of financial institutions in 2008.
bring up (raise)	The subject has been **brought up** several times in Parliamentary questions, but rarely receives a full debate.
call for something (make a public demand)	Three public sector unions have **called for** strike action if changes are not made to the programme of cuts.
call on/ for someone *to* ... (demand action)	Human rights activists **called on/for** the Government **to** impose economic sanctions on the regime.
set up (establish)	A panel of enquiry was **set up** to investigate the need for legislation in the area.
speak out about/against (speak publicly)	A number of protestors have **spoken out** about/against the treatment they received in prison.
take on (assume responsibility for)	A committee of MPs has **taken on** the task of overhauling outdated laws on computer hacking.

Exercises

1 Rewrite these sentences, replacing the underlined phrases with a more formal alternative.

1 It may take a small business more than a year to <u>get over</u> a quarterly fall in sales.
2 During the train strike, Enco plc <u>laid on</u> a special bus service to take employees from the factory to the head office.
3 A tier of middle managers were <u>laid off</u>, and six junior staff were appointed to replace them.
4 If the pressure becomes too acute, a manager may be tempted to <u>jack in</u> his job.
5 In times of recession, companies often <u>cut back on</u> seasonal and temporary staff.
6 Some consumers are likely to feel they are being <u>ripped off</u> if the monthly cost of calls rises dramatically after the trial period.
7 <u>Getting</u> your ideas <u>across</u> in a concise way is the key to success in a presentation.
8 A meeting was called in an attempt to <u>sort out</u> the dispute.

2 Rewrite these sentences, replacing the underlined word/phrases with a phrasal verb from this unit.

1 Stevens argued that a committee should be <u>formed</u> to consider new ways of protecting the users of social network sites from online bullying.
2 Some whistleblowers will <u>give their views in public</u> even when their jobs are clearly at risk.
3 According to Sorelson, the final report did not <u>take account of</u> the possibility that some of the evidence may have been contaminated.
4 After <u>reflecting on</u> the merits of both arguments, Polson concludes that further legislation did not offer a satisfactory way forward.
5 Barker <u>used</u> her experience in Kenya to argue for an international summit on the regulations governing the hunting of tigers.
6 The study <u>highlights</u> the need for further research.
7 Several prominent figures <u>openly requested</u> the Minister's resignation.
8 Errors in their statistics meant that their argument <u>was not credible</u>.

56   Commonly misused words

Some words have a tendency to be confused. This is usually because they have a similar form or sound, even though their meanings may differ.

The Cultural revolution was a **historic** event in China.	→	being or taking place in the past and becoming significant in history
The book provides a **historical** account of the events leading up to the Cultural Revolution.	→	based on an analysis of important events in history

💡 Writing Tip

Your spellchecker will not pick up errors with these words because the errors involve words that do exist but are being used wrongly. Learn the meaning and spelling of these words, incorporate them into your writing and make sure you use them correctly.

▶ Here are some examples of words that are commonly confused.

1 Words that are in the same general area of meaning

advice	the noun (a piece of advice)
advise	the verb (consultants who advise the government)

My ~~advise~~ **advice** is that you should learn when to use 'c' and when to use 's'.

affect	the verb (which will affect many people)
effect	the noun (which will have an effect on many people)

Changes in policy had a major ~~affect~~ **effect** on immigration numbers.

2 Words that have a different meaning

adverse	an adjective meaning *negative, not good* or *unhelpful* (adverse weather conditions)
averse	an adjective used with **to**, meaning *not liking* or *opposed to*

Older people are sometimes ~~adverse~~ **averse to** change.

allusion	a noun meaning *an indirect reference to something*
illusion	a noun meaning *a false idea or belief*

Patients were **under the** ~~allusion~~ **illusion that** the drug was making them better.

apprise	used in the pattern **apprise someone of something**, meaning *inform*
appraise	used with a noun, meaning *assess* or *evaluate* (appraise an employee)

The President was ~~appraised~~ **apprised of** the latest developments in the crisis.

censor	a verb or noun related to *censorship*
sensor	a noun used to describe a *device that senses change or presence*

The robot is fitted with ~~censors~~ **sensors** that can detect any obstacle in its path.

complementary	used to describe *features or characteristics that go together well*
complimentary	used to describe *praising someone or something*

Leadership and public speaking are ~~complimentary~~ **complementary** skills.

economic	an adjective meaning *relating to the economy* (an economic downturn)
economical	an adjective meaning *saving or not wasting money*

In a time of recession, many people are forced to adopt a more ~~economic~~ **economical** lifestyle.

insure	a verb linked to *insurance*
ensure	a verb meaning *make sure*
assure	a verb meaning *to remove any doubts someone may have about something*

We need to ~~insure~~ ~~assure~~ **ensure** that these materials are handled with care.

elicit	a verb meaning *to draw a reaction or opinion from someone*
illicit	an adjective used to refer to something that is *illegal*

The company's ~~elicit~~ **illicit** practices brought it to the attention of the authorities.

| eminent | an adjective that means *respected in your field* |
| imminent | an adjective that means *about to happen* |

Professor Jonathan White is an ~~imminent~~ **eminent** researcher in the field of biochemistry.

| emigrate | a verb used to refer to *people leaving a country to go to another one* |
| immigrate | a verb used to refer to *people entering a country from another one* |

In the 1950s and 60s many UK citizens ~~immigrated~~ **emigrated** to Australia.

NOTE: In the two examples above, the words beginning with 'i' have a double 'm'.

| imply | a verb used to *suggest something without saying it* |
| infer | a verb used to *deduce something that has not been directly stated* |

In his report, Dr Star ~~infers~~ **implies** that some of the council's recommendations are naive.

| incidence | a noun meaning *the frequency with which something happens* |
| incident | a noun meaning *an event or something that happens* |

During the recession, there was a higher ~~incidents~~ **incidence** of mental health problems among the population.

| loose | an adjective meaning *the opposite of tight* |
| lose | a verb meaning *the opposite of find or gain* |

During this period, Britain began to ~~loose~~ **lose** its influence in world affairs.

| refute | a verb meaning *to prove that a theory, opinion, idea, etc., is wrong* |
| reject | a verb meaning *to be unwilling to accept something* |

Simonds ~~refutes~~ rejects the notion that Dickens influenced our understanding of the social issues of his period.

Remember!

The phrases **regardless of** and **irrespective of** have the same meaning, but 'irregardless of' does not exist:
They went ahead with the plan, **regardless of/irrespective of/** ~~irregardless of~~ the high costs involved.

Danger Zone

Comprise / consist of / is composed of

'Comprise' is not followed by 'of':
The tool ~~comprises of~~ a metal grip, cutters and a probe. ✗
The tool **comprises** a metal grip, cutters and a probe.

'Consist' and 'be composed' are followed by 'of':
The tool **consists of** / **is composed of** a metal grip, cutters and a probe. ✔

Exercises

1 Choose the correct alternative in italics.

1 Net immigration figures take into account the number of *immigrants/emigrants* as well as the number of people coming into a country.

2 Once the peace talks had broken down, everyone realised that war was *eminent/ imminent*.

3 The organising body *assured/ensured/insured* participants that no-one would have an unfair advantage.

4 If he persists with the road-building scheme, the councillor will *lose/loose* his seat.

5 The author does not refer to herself; nevertheless, readers can *infer/imply* an autobiographical element.

6 The *economic/economical* history of the country from 1950 to 1975 is covered in the article.

7 Some very *complementary/complimentary* remarks were made during the prize-giving ceremony.

8 British Sign Language *is composed/comprises* of different signs from its American counterpart.

2 Use a word from this unit to complete the gaps in the paragraphs.

The installation of a piece of modern art has to be undertaken in consultation with those who live in the city and who will see it every day. Failure to do this has sometimes resulted in an unpleasant (1) ....
Of primary importance is the need to (2) .... the views of citizens prior to the installation. This will (3) .... that no one can say, at the end of the process, that they were not consulted. If the local council takes expert (4) .... and canvasses as many opinions as possible, it will find that this also has a positive (5) .... on relationships. People who are (6) ...... to the idea will be able to make their feelings clear and those responsible will be (7) ...... of what the general reaction is and act accordingly. The unveiling of a major work of art in a city should be a (8) ...... occasion enjoyed by all, rather than something that is seen as an unwelcome intrusion.

57 Commonly confused words – homonyms

Homonyms sound the same but are spelt differently, may be different parts of speech and may have different meanings.

As an author, she ~~new~~ **knew** exactly what she was capable of reproducing in prose.

adjective   verb (simple past form)

 Writing Tip

Homonyms are often simple, basic words and their confusion can result in serious errors. Often mistakes of this kind are the result of carelessness, so it is important to check your work before you hand it in.

▶ **Here are some examples of homonyms that are commonly confused.**

aloud / allowed
No collaboration was ~~aloud~~ **allowed** between the parties during the course of the investigation.

bear / bare
The freezing temperatures made living on the ~~bear~~ **bare** essentials even more challenging than usual. (= basic)
Councils had to ~~bare~~ **bear** the full costs of the scheme. (= supply / accept)
Local residents could not ~~bare~~ **bear** further noise from the airport. (= tolerate)

break / brake
At one point, there was serious concern that talks between the parties would ~~brake~~ **break** down but, fortunately, this did not happen.

born / borne
These doubts were ~~born~~ **borne out** by later events. (= proved correct)

counsel / council
The need to ~~council~~ **counsel** war veterans is much more widely accepted than it used to be. (= advise and support)
The ~~counsel~~ **council** failed to allocate sufficient funds to the project.

here / hear
More longitudinal studies are required on the impact of electronic noise on people's ability to ~~here~~ **hear**.

licence (noun) / license (verb)
A ~~license~~ **licence** is required for premises to have live music performances.
NOTE: In American English both the noun and verb are **license** with an 's'.

practice (noun) / practise (verb)
This is common ~~practise~~ **practice** in the industry.
To ~~practice~~ **practise** medicine in this country, you will need to pass a language test.
NOTE: In American English both the noun and verb are **practice** with a 'c'.

past / passed
Only three years have ~~past~~ **passed** since the disaster occurred.

principle (noun = belief) / principal (adjective = main; noun = head of educational institution)
Conservation is one of the ~~principle~~ **principal** concerns of biologists today.
He refused, on the grounds that it was against his ~~principals~~ **principles**.

site / sight
People demonstrated against the proposal to use the area as the ~~sight~~ **site** for a nuclear reactor.

to / too
Experts say that it is ~~to~~ **too** soon to predict the impact of eco-tourism projects on indigenous populations.

weather / whether
Several criteria must be taken into account when deciding ~~weather~~ **whether** or not to upgrade an existing building.

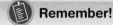 **Remember!**
The word 'wether' does not exist; whether is spelt with an 'h'.

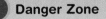

Remember!

Use **too** (not 'to') with the meanings 'more than is wanted':
The cost was ~~to~~ **too** high.

and 'also':
The plan was complex and it was very expensive ~~to~~ **too**.

! Danger Zone

its/it's

its is a possessive: They discussed the organisation of the project and its costs.
it's = 'it is'   It's a difficult problem to solve.
Problems with ~~it's~~ **its infrastructure** held the country back.

there/their/they're

there is the subject of a verb: and there were several unforeseen consequences
their is a possessive   older people and their needs
they're = they are   and they're all serious issues
The children's developmental problems were said to be linked to ~~there~~ **their diet**.
People have looked for solutions but ~~there~~ **they're hard** to find.

your/you're

your is a possessive   fill in your details below
you're = you are   you're making a mistake
I'm glad that ~~your~~ **you're going** to work with me on this.

who's/whose

who's = who is/who has   the person who's in charge of the office
whose is a possessive   someone whose judgement I trust
Dickens is a writer ~~who's~~ **whose novels** continue to be read by millions.

Exercises

1 Six of these sentences contain a mistake. Find the mistakes and correct them.

1 Unlike many laws of physics, Archimedes Principal is over two thousand years old.
2 Actions that had been agreed at the strategy meeting turned out to be to costly to implement.
3 A clear distinction has to be made between pushing the boundaries and actually breaking them.
4 The biodiversity reserve has aloud previously threatened plant species to survive.
5 Problems such as dyslexia often past unnoticed in the 1960s.
6 Candidates were advised to submit applications as quickly as possible to be sure of a place.
7 Not knowing weather to save money or invest it is a common problem these days.
8 Perfectionists often cannot bare to be criticised.

2 Correct the ten mistakes in this paragraph.

One of the problems that arises when your paying for something over the internet is that you never see whose receiving your details at the other end. We like to think that their trustworthy but its impossible to know wether that is the case. As anyone whose been the victim of credit card fraud will know, it can very difficult to regain you're faith in online shopping once your identity has been stolen. Shops and restaurants may seem safer but just as much fraud goes on their as it does on the web. These days, customers need reassurance that their transactions are safe and banks need to raise there game with regard to financial security. For all it's advantages, the online world can certainly have its downside.

58   Key spelling rules

Words are made up of **vowels** (a, e, i, o, u) and **consonants** (b, c, d, etc.).
Some words, such as **phenomenon**, are hard to spell and there are often no rules to help you.
Other words have **prefixes** and/or **suffixes** (e.g. **in**sensiti**vity**) and their spelling may adhere to certain rules.

> 💡 **Writing Tip**
>
> Although English spelling can be difficult, try to remember some of the rules as they will help you correct or avoid mistakes. However, bear in mind that the rules often have exceptions.

▶ Here are some spelling rules for adding suffixes and verb endings to words.

Words ending in 'e'

- **lose the final 'e'**
  if the suffix begins with a vowel or 'ing' is added

visible	→	visibility	abbreviate	→	abbreviation
refuse	→	refusal	undeniable	→	undeniably
insure	→	insurance	suffice	→	sufficient
intrigue	→	intriguing	write	→	writing

  Exceptions include some 'able' adjectives, such as knowledgeable, likeable.
  This rule is not true for words ending 'ee', e.g. guaranteeing, freeing

- **keep the final 'e'**
  if the suffix begins with a consonant or 'd' is added

  objective → objectively   define → defined
  inventive → inventiveness
  Exceptions include truly and argument.

Words ending in 'y'

- **change the final 'y' to 'ie'**
  if 'ed' is added to a verb that ends in a consonant + 'y'

  comply → complied   verify → verified
  Keep the 'y' if you are adding 'ing' (complying; verifying).

  if 'er' or 'est' are added to an adjective

  meaty → meatier   lively → liveliest

  if plural 's' is added to a noun

  contemporary → contemporaries   reality → realities
  opportunity → opportunities   theory → theories

- **to form an adverb, change 'y' to 'ily'**

  funny → funnily   temporary → temporarily

- **do not change the final 'y'**
  if 'ed' or 'ing' are added to a verb that ends in a vowel + 'y'

  portray → portrayed   convey → conveying

Words ending in a consonant

- **double the final consonant**
  if the word ends in one vowel + consonant

  plan → planned   slip → slippery   plot → plotting
  big → biggest   deter → deterrent   upset → upsetting

Exceptions include words ending in 'c' (this often becomes 'ck': panicking); words ending in 'w' (growing), 'x' (fixed) and 'y' (stayed).

If the word ends with two vowels and a consonant, as in 'great' → greatest, the letter is not usually doubled.

if the word ends in vowel + 'l'

virtual	→	virtually	logical →	logically
instil	→	instilling	appal →	appalled

Exceptions include fulfil → fulfilment

Note also these words ending 'er'

prefer → prefe<u>rr</u>ing → prefe<u>r</u>ence
refer → refe<u>rr</u>ing → refe<u>r</u>ence

and words ending 'it'

commit → commi<u>tt</u>ed → commi<u>t</u>ment → commi<u>tt</u>ee
elicit → elicited → eliciting
exhibit → exhibited → exhibiting

♦ See **50** *Adjectives and adverbs* and **53** *Using longer words*.

> **Remember!**
> When 'ful' is used as a suffix, it never has double 'l' – successful, plentiful, awful.

Adding a prefix

- Adding a prefix does not usually change the spelling of a word, although it may necessitate the addition of a hyphen.
- If the last letter of the prefix is the same as the first letter of a word, the new word you form will have a double letter:

misrepresented *but* mis**s**pelled   **in**valuable *but* in**n**umerable

disassociate *but* disservice   **un**educated *but* un**n**ecessary

NOTE: 'il' and 'ir' are only added to words that begin with 'l' and 'r' so the letter is always doubled: **il**logical / **il**literate / **ir**relevant / **ir**refutable

Exercise

1 Correct the spelling of these words using the rules in this unit.

1 controling
2 diarys
3 missquoted
4 hygieneic

5 delightfull
6 iregular
7 bidable
8 dissapointed

2 Change the words in brackets into the correct form by adding a prefix, suffix or verb ending.

1 ………. (open) to change can represent a significant …….. (improve) in people diagnosed with Obsessive Compulsive Disorder.

2 The institution is ……… (primary) concerned with rehabilitation following a ……. (stress) illness.

3 Greater levels of ……… (co-operate) between staff and local governing bodies have led to ……. (notice) improvements in care.

4 The controversy arose because ministers' ……. (argue) had been …….. (construe).

5 The ……… (set) up of a respite care system marked an important ……. (achieve) for all concerned.

6 The study reflected on the ……… (continuity) of care and their effect on youngsters …….. (await) adoption.

7 Strategies used to encourage the prescription of drugs developed by selected pharmaceutical ……. (company) should be …….. (prohibit).

8 Researchers are aware that the social …….. (behave) of some patients with mental health problems is not overly …….. (similar) to that of healthy people.

59 Common spelling mistakes

▶ **Read this paragraph from an essay on English literature and think about which words have been spelled wrongly.**

Jane Austen's novel *Pride and Prejudice* was, it seems, quiet carefully constructed. It makes a clear statement about moral values at the time she was writting, yet also has a timeless significance. Unlike some of her contempories, she restricted herself to the type of world she knew she was capable of reproducing in prose. She understood her own social enviroment and never went beyond this. As a result, the story presents a snapshot of 18th-century life, without exagerration or extremes. She insured that any detail was kept to a mininum. A close examination of the descriptive passages reveals little in the way of figurative language; few similes or metaphors; no extraenous emotion. The reader can be secure in the knowledge that there will be no distractions from the all-important plot.

Wm. Shakespeare aged 7

Alas, poor Yorick! I new him well

Teacher: See me!

• Here are some of the reasons why spelling mistakes occur:

1 **Some words have silent letters or letters that don't get clearly pronounced:**

'She understood her own social ~~enviroment~~ **environment** and never went beyond this.'
Here are some more examples:

~~goverment~~	government	~~religous~~	religious
~~exibit~~	exhibit	~~densly~~	densely
~~psycology~~	psychology	~~assinement~~	assignment
~~neigbour~~	neighbour	~~garantee~~	guarantee

2 **Some words are not spelt the way they sound:**

Unlike some of her ~~contempories~~ **contemporaries**, she restricted herself to the type of world she knew she was capable of reproducing in prose.
Here are some more examples:

~~dependant~~	dependent	~~tempory~~	temporary
~~summery~~	summary	~~responsability~~	responsibility
~~definately~~	definitely	~~persue~~	pursue
~~seperate~~	separate	~~ditract~~	detract

3 **Some words have a challenging mix of single and double letters:**

'As a result, the story presents a snapshot of 18th-century life, without ~~exagerration~~ **exaggeration** or extremes.'
Here are some more examples:

~~acomodation~~	accommodation	~~appartment~~	apartment
~~inovation~~	innovation	~~asessment~~	assessment
~~abreviate~~	abbreviate	~~ocasion~~	occasion
~~fullfillment~~	fulfilment	~~embarass~~	embarrass
~~reccomend~~	recommend	~~necesary~~	necessary

4 Some words have vowel or consonant groups that pose problems:

'A close examination of the descriptive passages reveals little in the way of figurative language; few similes or metaphors; no ~~extraenous~~ **extraneous** emotion.'

Here are some more examples:

~~reciept~~	receipt	~~rythm~~	rhythm
~~hygeine~~	hygiene	~~pharoah~~	pharaoh
~~diareah~~	diarrhoea	~~langauge~~	language
~~twelth~~	twelfth	~~syncronise~~	synchronise

> **Remember!**
>
> The rhyme: *'i' before 'e' except after 'c'* holds true for most words: receive, perceive, believe, reprieve, conceive.
> Exceptions include weird, weigh and neighbour.

5 Some words are commonly confused or misused:

'Jane Austen's novel *Pride and Prejudice* was, it seems, ~~quiet~~ **quite** carefully constructed.'

She ~~insured~~ **ensured** that any detail was kept to a mininum

♦ See **56** *Commonly misused words* and **57** *Commonly confused words.*

6 Some words are spelt differently when their form changes:

'It makes a clear statement about moral values at the time she was ~~writting~~ **writing**, yet also has a timeless significance.'   ♦ See **53** *Using longer words.*

American versus British spelling

Many institutions accept American or British spelling but whichever you use, it is important to be consistent. Common examples of differences include:

American	British	American	British	American	British
color	colour	centre	center	connexion	connection
fulfill	fulfil	catalog	catalogue	kilometer	kilometre

- Some words ending in 'ise'; e.g. organise, criticise, publicise are spelt with a 'z' in American English: organize, criticize, publicize. Many others, however, are not.

Exercises

1 Decide which of the words is misspelt and write the correct spelling in the second column.

1	wierd		6	oppotunities	
2	necesary		7	excellence	
3	comittment		8	access	
4	integrated		9	successfull	
5	stabalise		10	concieve	

2 Each line in the paragraph contains one spelling mistake: underline it and write the correct word in the space provided.

	Corrections
Graham Greene was an acomplished novelist of the 1930s. Although	
many of his books have a religous significance, he also caught the	
mood of his day, unlike many of his contempories who only gave a	
very faint idea of the harsh realaties of life under the shadows of war.	
Greene's knowlede and understanding of his society were drawn	
primerily from newspapers and, in this way he was able to produce	
realistic caracters, rather than relying on fictional creations. Today	
he remains a much-loved writer whose tendency to potray life	
in somewhat pesimistic terms does not detract in any way from	
his overall appeal.	

60 Writing an email to your tutor

Like any other form of communication, an **email** should be written with the reader in mind.

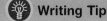 **Writing Tip**

An email will create a positive or negative impression on your tutor, depending on how it is written. However well you get on with your tutor, your correspondence should reflect your relative status, should be clear and easy to read and should not contain mistakes.

Write a clear and useful subject line

Your tutor is a busy person and has an inbox full of emails. He or she needs to be able to quickly note the content of a message and make any necessary response.

```
Subject: Hi!
```
```
Subject: Need a favour please!
```
```
Subject: Quick question
```

What's wrong: At a glance, none of the subject lines gives any indication of what the email is about.

● Here is an example of a full, clear subject line.

```
Subject: Request work reference for Dave Watts, History 2006
```

Remember!

Your email address may bear no relation to your name so putting your name in the subject line may be helpful if your tutor has a lot of students. It may be useful to add your course details as well.

● Here are some further guidelines.

Use correct grammar

Contractions (e.g. won't) are acceptable, but grammatical mistakes, even in a short message, can cause confusion and annoy the reader.

▶ **Find six grammatical errors in this email and add an appropriate subject line.**

```
Subject: ...............................

I'm really sorry but I'll be late handing in my assignment on care of the
elderly. The due date's 27th of this month and I know I should of finished by
then but I wonder if I hand it in a week later. I've been off sick with a really
bad throat infection and didn't have time to do all the reading yet. I'd like to
ask for a week's extension, would give me time to catch up. I hope my term grades
isn't affected by this.

Tony Hill
```

Punctuate your email

A well-punctuated email is much easier to read than a poorly punctuated one.

▶ **Insert six punctuation marks in this email and make two additional changes.**

```
Ive just started the module on world Archaeology (3033) and am finding the topic
a bit too broad. I realise that although I like the global coverage I would
be better suited to something more specific as I've always had an interest in
African Archaeology could I change to this module.
```

NOTE: You don't have to use formal punctuation (e.g. semi-colons) in emails, although many people do.

Make clear connections within sentences

Unnecessary repetition and inaccurate referencing should be avoided in emails.

▶ Replace the underlined words so that the connections are improved, and write an appropriate subject line.

> Subject: ....
>
> I've decided to take part in the Mongol Rally next year, <u>it</u> involves driving a car from Europe to Mongolia over the summer vacation. I wonder if you could sponsor me for <u>the Mongol Rally</u>. It's not a race and I'm not trying to win anything – <u>that's</u> all about making it to the end of the route and donating your vehicle to a local charity. I've always admired <u>them</u> people who take on a charitable cause, so I've decided to have a go at <u>these</u> myself. Can I count on your support?

Make sure your sentences can be understood

You must ensure that everything you write makes clear sense.

▶ Rewrite this email so that the sentences are correct and complete.

> I'd like to change the topic for my presentation. I did say that I would do it on communication issues. Have previously worked on this. But I've found it very hard to find enough material or getting the right ideas. Now I think I have a better idea that I've been working on if it's ok if I do it on sensory deprivation instead?

Make sure style and function are appropriate

Although emails are informal, you should avoid using slang or poor expression when writing to your tutor.

▶ Underline four words/phrases in this email that you think should be replaced.

> Subject: Re our appointment
>
> I've just realised that I should have been in a meeting with you this morning! I dunno why I forgot but I feel really bad about it. I'd like to re-schedule the meeting if possible cos I still have some problems with my presentation. What about Friday at 10?

Remember!

Read your email through before you send it. Like any other piece of writing, you won't get it right first time.

Use appropriate words and correct spelling

Like grammar mistakes, errors in vocabulary create a bad impression.

▶ Find eight mistakes in word choice or spelling in this email.

> I've just applied for a job as a volunteer in a charity shop and I need to provide the names of two people who know me but who aren't relatives. I'd really apreciate it if I could put you're name down as a reference. I think they'll contact you and it only involvs writing a short paragraph about me, outlining my skills and giving some information about my caracter. I don't think there's any point of writing a lot as it's only a tempory job.
>
> Could I also contact you for advise if I get an interview?

Key

1 Parts of speech

Exercise 1

noun: course, qualification, graduates, positions, variety, professions, details, website, advice, service, students, answers, queries

verb: provides, find, are, operate, can, get

adjective: useful, Full, available, prospective, clear

adverb: regularly, quickly

preposition: in, of, on, to

article: The, a, a, an

pronoun: our, we, their

linking: and, In addition, so that

Exercise 2

1 E
2 C
3 F
4 D
5 C
6 G
7 B
8 A

2 Parts of a sentence

Exercise 1

b There is no main verb with 'Education' (the subject). The main verb should be 'has been'.

Exercise 2

1 subject: pupils; main verb: can take; object: the International Baccalaureate
2 subject: many people; main verb: welcomed; object: comprehensive schools
3 subject: selective schools; main verb: require; object: candidates

Exercise 3

1 Students applying for university places have to complete the application process, which includes a personal statement.
2 The three categories of state schools during the 1960s were grammar, comprehensive and secondary modern.
3 In the 1990s, when polytechnics changed their name and became universities, the overall number of applications for higher education places rose sharply.

Exercise 4

1 Three clauses:
   main clause: The system for the funding of higher education is a major issue in the UK
   other clauses: which has changed several times over the past few decades
   affecting a great many families.
2 Three clauses:
   main clause: British universities have long attracted overseas students
   other clauses: because of their high reputation and these students have become an important source of revenue.
3 Two clauses:
   main clause: the variety of courses on offer at British universities has greatly increased over the last two decades
   other clause: in order to attract students who otherwise may not have gone to a university at all.

3 Singular/plural subjects & verbs

Exercise 1

1 ✓ ('government' is a group noun used here to refer to a single unit)
2 ✗ (the subject is the plural 'issues')
3 ✗ (the subject is the plural 'Problems')
4 ✗ (the subject is the plural 'people')
5 ✓ (the subject is the plural 'developments')
6 ✓ (the subject is the singular 'result').
7 ✗ (the subject is the plural 'repercussions')

Exercise 2

1 thinks
2 tend
3 suffer
4 were
5 has
6 surround
7 were

4 Correct tense formation

Exercise 1

1 ✓
2 ✗ became
3 ✗ have supported
4 ✓

5

6 ❌ realised

Exercise 2

1 has
2 were
3 liked
4 had been using
5 wore
6 owned
7 had bought
8 were using
9 have become
10 have been attracting

5 Using more than one verb tense

Exercise 1

1 ✔
2 ❌ had analysed
3 ❌ could understand
4 ✔
5 ✔
6 ❌ had come

Exercise 2

1 fish were returning to the river now that it was unpolluted.
2 he would stay in office until the board had appointed a successor
3 they were investigating the problem but had not found the cause yet.
4 the talks had been successful and they hoped to sign an agreement.
5 until exports rose, economic growth would not return.
6 she could not comment because she did not know the details of the case.

6 Modal verbs

Exercise 1

1 did not need to open
2 had to release
3 cannot
4 need not have resigned.
5 must have been working
6 should

Exercise 2

1 ❌ Dalio's work in sculpture **could not/cannot have been** a success because she soon turned to painting.

2 ✔ ('could' describes a lifetime skill, not a specific achievement)
3 ❌ With a more attractive design, the product **could have become** a brand leader.
4 ❌ Critics argued that the gallery **ought not to have allowed** the painting to be sold to a museum.
5 ❌ Fortunately, the organisers **were able to save/managed to save/succeeded in saving** the show by using a back-up generator.
6 ✔

7 Using the passive

Exercise 1

1 The Nobel Peace Prize was won by former American President Jimmy Carter in 2002.
2 The Bill will be debated (by MPs) later in the week.
3 The documents were being destroyed (by a clerk) when the police arrived.
4 The referendum might be postponed (by the Government).
5 Three government buildings have been occupied by protestors.
6 Most of the museum's collection had been stolen by rioters by the time the army arrived.

Exercise 2

1 It is believed that Walter Clark is the Senate's most skilful debater.
   Walter Clark is believed to be the Senate's most skilful debater.
2 It was reported that two politicians took bribes for their votes.
   Two politicians were reported to have taken bribes for their votes.
3 It is said that talks are taking place between the two parties.
   Talks are said to be taking place between the two parties.
4 It is thought that Che Guevara was executed to avoid the drama of a trial.
   Che Guevara is thought to have been executed to avoid the drama of a trial.

8 Direct & indirect questions

Exercise 1

1 ❌ It was hard for legislators at the time to foresee **what the effects of this law would be.**
2 ✔

3 ✓

4 ✗ Experts need to co-operate in order to determine exactly **how a new law can be implemented/how to implement a new law.**

5 ✗ Many professionals are still finding out **how the internet affects them** from a professional point of view.

6 ✓

7 ✗ The public should be clear about **whether or not they have broken** the law.

Exercise 2

1 We have to ask ourselves **why such a law is required.**

2 It is hard to be exact about **when this problem first arose.**

3 It would be useful to know **what the origins of this law were / how this law originated.**

4 People are asking **how quickly the law can be implemented.**

5 We have to decide **in what areas / where we should implement this law.**

6 The public is asking **what other laws will be needed in the future.**

7 People need to know **whether they have broken** the law.

9 Conditionals (If …)

Exercise 1

1 If Techgames had increased their prices, they would have lost their share of the youth market.

2 Bailey Ltd might not have failed/might have succeeded if they had used internet marketing.

3 The sales team could have won new orders if they had attended the trade fair in Barcelona.

4 If the advertising campaign had focused on young professionals, it would have succeeded.

5 If it had not diversified five years ago, Longgame plc would not be flourishing today.

Exercise 2

1 But for
2 Had the
3 Had it
4 Even if
5 If it

Exercise 3

1 ✓

2 ✗ If video links were **to** replace trade fairs, sales teams would lose the vital link with retailers in the places where they live and work.

3 ✓

4 ✗ If **it** were not for Goldsworth's successful Paris branch, the company would be making a loss.

5 ✓

6 ✗ Provided that it continues to innovate, the company has a bright future.

10 Time words and phrases

Exercise 1

1 are yet to be implemented
2 only to regret it later
3 on the verge of finding a cure for the disease
4 had still to emerge
5 in the process of reforming the system
6 proved to have been a very good one
7 on the point of resigning
8 was soon to improve
9 was to have unforeseen consequences

Exercise 2

1 Industrial relations were reaching an all-time low in the 1970s. Meanwhile, overseas competitors were flourishing.

2 The country was developing economically. Meanwhile, it was also changing culturally.

Exercise 3

1 ✗ any more/longer / was no longer relevant
2 ✗ weren't expensive for most people any more/longer / were no longer expensive for most people
3 ✓
4 ✓

11 Emphasising

Exercise 1

1 It was the one-way system that was making the situation worse.

2 What visitors to Scotland enjoy most is its magnificent scenery.

3 Only by purchasing local produce can/will consumers reduce the amount of food transportation.

4 What people want is easy access to the main tourist sites.

5 It is value for money rather than luxury that most passengers seek in an airline operator.

6 Only by retaining their essential character can/will resorts attract tourism in the long term.

Exercise 2

1 undoubtedly
2 whatsoever
3 itself
4 indeed
5 entirely

12 Negative expressions and structures

Exercise 1

1 ✅
2 ❌ either
3 ❌ nor
4 ✅
5 ❌ anything
6 ❌ was it

Exercise 2

1 No sooner had people become accustomed to the situation than it changed.
2 No matter how quickly they worked, they could not keep up with demand.
3 Hardly had she got rid of one reporter when another one appeared.
4 On no account could the policy be allowed to fail.
5 It was only when inflation started to rise that people began to worry about the economy.
6 Not until recent times has this been considered an important issue.

Exercise 3 (suggested answers)

1 The policy didn't fail/wasn't a failure but it wasn't particularly successful either.
2 This is something that can be explained fairly easily. / This isn't something that is difficult to explain.
3 Most voters felt that the election result was a foregone conclusion. / Not many voters doubted that the election result was a foregone conclusion.

13 Gerunds & infinitives

Exercise 1

1 introducing; to draft
2 restructuring; to finalising
3 to implement; carrying
4 losing; to changing
5 to improve; not to have
6 to believe; changing
7 making; having

8 to increasing; recruiting

Exercise 2

One of the major problems of his period as Prime Minister was that he could not admit **to making** any mistakes. Aides urged him to do so, on the grounds that it would make the public **think** differently about him. They told him that the public expected their leaders to show a human side but he refused **to take** any notice of their advice. He would not consider altering his approach and he denied having an image that the public found off-putting. Accustomed **to having** his own way, he resented **being** told that he needed to make concessions to public opinion. For two more years, he tried to justify continuing in the same old way, but eventually the voters had their say.

Exercise 3

1 To avoid
2 Getting
3 finding
4 to ensure

14 Articles (a/an, the)

Exercise 1

1 For most parents, education is one of the biggest sources of concern with regard to their children.
2 ✅
3 Despite spending large amounts of money, the government did not manage to achieve its targets for health care.
4 It has been argued that people now have higher expectations of life and that this can cause them unhappiness.

Exercise 2

1 In 1955, he travelled to India and, on his return, he wrote an emotional account of the experiences he had had on the journey.
2 Towards the end of the 20th century, the lives of many people in developed countries were transformed by the arrival of computer technology.
3 Suddenly, the entire industry changed and a new approach was required to the whole area of marketing.
4 There wasn't an obvious solution to the problem and opinions varied as to what the best course of action was.

5 Many people claim in surveys that job satisfaction is more important than a high salary.

Exercise 3

It became clear that <u>the</u> further research was required and the two people who carried this out were faced with the problem of how best to do it. After <u>the</u> discussions, they decided that the focus of the research should be <u>the</u> attitudes to <u>the</u> happiness because they wanted to focus on the effect of <u>the</u> increased prosperity on <u>the</u> modern society. Having decided on this, they set out to find the kind of subjects that would best suit their purpose.

15 Relative clauses (who, which, that, etc.)

Exercise 1

1 ✗ Much research has been conducted into schizophrenia, *which* causes chronic behavioural problems.
2 ✓
3 ✗ Newton and Einstein are considered to be the scientists to *whom* modern physics owes the greatest debt.
4 ✗ Water, which is regarded as evidence of life, may have existed relatively recently on the surface of Mars.
5 ✓

Exercise 2

1 A number of questions were asked about the equipment that/which was used in the experiment.
2 The Jodrell Bank Observatory, which was established in 1945, has played an important part in researching meteors, pulsars and quasars.
3 John Nash made some of the key early insights into modern game theory, which led to his being co-awarded the Nobel Prize in 1994.
4 Michael Faraday was a scientist whose research into magnetic fields gained him his reputation.
5 During the lecture the audience were introduced to Margaret Simons, who had first identified two of the species of spider being discussed.

Exercise 3

1 in which
2 to whom, to which
3 after/for whom

16 Comparing and contrasting

Exercise 1

1 Staff development opportunities are less important to factory employees than clear lines of communication.
2 Raw materials can be transported more quickly by train than by road.
3 British businesses are not spending as much as European companies on product design, according to recent studies.
4 The French engines were heavier than the replacements from Germany.
5 Export results are as impressive as import figures this year.
6 The safety systems were checked less regularly than they should have been.

Exercise 2

1 Kenton was asked to design a vehicle that would operate in the **wettest** conditions.
2 It was not as effective **a** system as the manufacturers had hoped.
3 ✓
4 Generally speaking, there are **fewer** opportunities for apprenticeships these days.
5 If the parts are cooled by water, the process can be completed **sooner**.
6 ✓
7 Some of the world's most desirable cars are criticised for also being the **least** fuel-efficient.
8 The workforce agreed that a shift system was the **safest** way of working.

17 Describing similarities and differences

Exercise 1

1 far
2 just
3 twice
4 one of
5 at least

Exercise 2

1 Similarly
2 differ
3 on the contrary
4 in common
5 In contrast

Exercise 3 (sample answer)

Lions and tigers have a number of characteristics in common. The two species are alike, for example, in that the females of both have a gestation period of around 100 days, although the average litter size of the lion is slightly larger (four cubs compared with the tiger's three). The female tiger also differs from the lion in terms of the length of time it spends nursing its young; while lionesses typically stop after eleven months, tigresses may suckle their cubs for more than twice as long a period. Both sets of cubs are similar, however, in reaching their sexual maturity at around 40 months.

18 Using noun phrases

Exercise 1

1 The **construction of** a one-way system will allow the council to reduce city-centre traffic.
2 The chairperson questioned the **relevance of** some of the research.
3 Local people greeted the announcement **with fury**.
4 There have been **improvements in** the town's provision of cheaper housing in recent years.
5 The **specially adapted** arena will host the athletics contest.
6 House prices have risen in the **rapidly expanding** suburbs.

Exercise 2

1 Because of the likelihood that residents would object, the proposal was withdrawn.
2 The council made final changes to the carefully-planned celebrations.
3 Local councillors understood the importance of the theatre to the town.
4 The widely-held view was that the council had acted too slowly.

Exercise 3

1 The warning that the bridge was about to collapse <u>was ignored</u> by the council.
2 The editor was dismissive of <u>the claim</u> that newspaper reports had exaggerated the costs of repairing the town hall.
3 The possibility that no funding <u>might be found</u> for the museum was finally accepted by the curator and her colleagues.
4 There were complaints when the rule <u>that</u> all councillors had to publish their expenses online was changed.
5 It was midnight before the statement that the Mayor <u>would resign</u> was read out.

19 Commas 1 – correct uses

On July 20th, 1969, having stepped onto the Moon's surface, Neil Armstrong uttered the famous words, 'One small step for man, one giant leap for mankind.' Although it had been hoped that the moon landing would lead to significant advances in space travel, some of which may soon become a reality, the scientific progress has generally been slow. However, space research has done much to unite nations. The establishment of the International Space Station, the Space Shuttle and the Hubble Telescope illustrates how much easier and more profitable it is for nations to work as a team, rather than in isolation.

20 Commas 2 – incorrect uses

Exercise 1

1 Professor Granger and his team presented the results of their research on the use of support staff in the classroom.
2 ✅
3 ✅
4 In the lower streams, on the other hand, there is little motivation amongst teachers to encourage students to do better, with the inevitable result that they fail to progress.
5 ✅
6 Course dates for some subjects have changed. You can find the changes on the relevant website.
7 Students can submit the application form online or by mail.

Exercise 2

1 As part of the course, you will analyse the theoretical ideas of socialism, conservatism and liberalism.
2 The Education Authority, realising that primary and secondary schools in some areas had too many applicants, devised a new admissions policy.
3 As the education plan proved to be flawed, impractical and unprofitable, it was quickly abandoned.
4 The Government has announced that students who live in rented accommodation may be eligible for financial assistance, whatever their circumstances.
5 'Labelling', the act of saying that a child is of a certain type, usually works to a child's disadvantage.

Exercise 3

According to this week's media, in particular the mainstream newspapers, class sizes in some British schools in the City of London are too big for Head Teachers to cope with and, as a consequence, some children are not fulfilling their academic potential. As a result of pressure from professionals in education, the Mayor has ordered an official enquiry into the situation, which will be run by Generating Genius, a charitable organisation that has already helped some teenagers from poorer socio-economic backgrounds to get good university places. The enquiry, which will take place over the next ten months, will look into a range of educational issues, including overcrowding in classrooms, improving overall standards, and promoting relationships between state and independent schools. On 12th November, the Mayor will speak at the Institute of Education, Bedford where, in the words of one reporter, 'there will be considerable interest in what he has to say'. In the meantime, in order to ensure that class sizes do not get out of hand, it is possible that the Greater London Authority will take steps to alleviate the situation by, for example, allocating some of its own buildings to the education of its city's young people.

21 Colons & semi-colons

Exercise 1

1 The report focuses on three issues: how reliable public transport systems are; what measures would be most effective in reducing traffic congestion; and whether parking facilities are adequate.
2 Most reports on the inner city focus on problems; in fact there have been many improvements too.
3 This leads us to another very important development in town planning: the arrival of out-of-town shopping centres.
4 Tomlinson was correct when he made the statement: 'Urban planners should always aim to avoid demolishing historic buildings'.
5 Among town planners today, there is one buzzword: sustainability.

Exercise 2

1 ✗ This brings me to my final point: the repercussions of local government initiatives have not always been carefully considered.

2 ✓
3 The drive to create a sustainable environment raises a serious question: to what extent should function take precedence over form?
4 People who argue that cities are becoming overcrowded should ask themselves why.
5 In some societies, homes need to be built to accommodate a range of family structures that include extended families, nuclear families and single-parent households.

22 Hyphens, dashes and brackets

Exercise 1

1 This was a <u>well-received</u> reform at the time. Prior to it, only <u>upper-class</u> people had been able to vote.
2 The records were not up to date and an <u>old-fashioned</u> system was still in place.
3 His <u>co-defendant</u> in the case was his former boss, and after a <u>three-month</u> trial, they were both found guilty.
4 By the time he was thirty years old, he had a <u>high-powered</u> job advising the government on <u>state-run</u> services.
5 Countries wanted <u>self-determination</u> and the status of being fully independent.

Exercise 2

1 Opponents questioned the logic of his argument – much to his annoyance.
2 He made a speech in the House of Commons – and this was not the only time when he went against his own party – in which he heavily criticised the policy.
3 Mistakes were made, inefficiency dogged the entire project, and complaints came in from all sides – this was not how things were supposed to be.
4 Pensioners – regardless of their personal and financial circumstances – were all better off because of this change.

Exercise 3

1 There were exceptions to this pattern but the results were generally very consistent. (Exceptions are listed in the table below.) It was therefore possible to draw firm conclusions.
2 He was a strong supporter of entry into the eurozone and played a significant role in the country's decision to take that step. (He later regretted this but that was far in the future.)

3 In her influential report (Approaches to Poverty, 2005), Browne proposed wholesale changes to welfare rules.

4 The unforeseen consequence (fewer workers having job security) seriously affected morale in the industry.

23 Apostrophes

Exercise 1

1 The beneficial effect of Vitamin D on **children's** health has been noted in recent research findings.

2 Apparently **Ferrari's** latest supercar can reach speeds of over 200 miles per hour.

3 The development of **teenagers'** identities is heavily influenced by their **peers'** behaviour.

4 People have enjoyed **Beethoven's** music for more than 200 years.

5 **I've** always believed that a **designer's** most successful approach is to follow his intuition, rather than pander to **clients'** ideas.

Exercise 2

1 Sales of **DVDs** rose rapidly during the period, and **their** ascendancy over **videos** was soon confirmed.

2 Cinema-going reached its height in the **1940s**, when its escapist appeal attracted audiences wanting to see movie stars **whose** lives seemed incredibly glamorous.

3 In some **experts'** views, the **EU's** target of 10 per cent biofuel use by 2020 is over-ambitious.

4 Boeing 747s are among the most commonly used commercial aircraft, and many **millions** of travellers have used them.

5 Research into people in their **20s** indicates that **theirs** is the first generation to be confronted by this problem, and many of them **can't** find a way to deal with it.

24 Inverted commas

Exercise 1

1 ✗ 'There are many different ways of accessing the information‚' the manual stated.

2 ✗ In a letter to his family, he wrote: 'I am beginning to think that perhaps the artistic life is not for me‚'

3 ✓

4 ✗ 'Why do certain people have these behaviour patterns?‚' she asks at the beginning of her paper.

5 ✓

6 ✗ One expert stated that the situation 'would not improve significantly ... for a considerable period of time'.

Exercise 2

1 In his paper 'The Impact of the Internet', he argued that too little attention was being paid to what he called 'the sudden intrusion'. By this he meant the speed at which the internet took over people lives. 'These days,' he said, 'people have lost the ability to think for themselves and to use their own initiative.'

2 Organisations often describe themselves in their own literature as being 'open and accountable'. One company I looked at in this research used the term 'open accountability' when discussing this issue. But what do companies mean by this?

3 After the first day of conference, the leaders announced in their official statement: 'We feel that we have made significant progress towards a solution on this difficult question.' They also spoke of the 'extremely cordial relations we enjoy'. 'We anticipate a further announcement after tomorrow's negotiations,' they added.

25 Capital letters

Exercise

1 The **Amazon** rainforest is two-thirds the size of the **US**, yet home to more than 30 million people and one in ten of the **Earth's** species.

2 Due to the screening of the **Mexican Grand Prix**, this week's quiz show, '**Send Me a Line**', will be broadcast on ITV at the earlier time of 5.00pm on **Friday**.

3 Farmers in the **Ivory Coast** barely make a living, while the cocoa produced there feeds the world's chocolate industry.

4 The folk artist, **Steve Knightley**, mixes music and legend on his latest **CD**, '**Cruel River**'.

5 In his book, **The End** of **Poverty**, **Jeffrey D. Sachs** looks at how some of the world's poorest people can improve their standard of living.

6 To go to university in **North America**, it is better to take the **International Baccalaureate** than A-Levels.

7 The flood seriously affected homes in the north-west of England and completely destroyed the 100-year-old premises of **Grandacre** and **Sons** in **Preston**.

8 Last week, the **UK Border Agency** announced that it would be making a number of changes in line with government policy.

9 The **Renaissance** was a period just before the **Modern Era** when great developments took place across **Europe** in art and literature.

10 In her paper, '**Talking** in **Twos**', **Amanda Pritchard** examines a new approach to raising bilingual children.

26 Linking: contrasting

Exercise 1

1 *Whilst* the number of annual visitors to the Galapagos Islands was 41,000 in 1991, it is now around 170,000.

2 *Despite* optimistic economic predictions, business confidence has fallen over the past few months.
Business confidence has fallen over the past few months, *despite* optimistic economic predictions.

3 Weather data has been collected in Britain for 350 years. *However*, opinions differ on how reliable that data is.
Opinions differ, *however*, on how reliable that data is.
Opinions differ on how reliable that data is, *however*.

4 *Even though* a dispersant was sprayed onto the oil slick, thousands of seabirds were washed up along the beach.

5 Some businesses invest heavily in researching new products, *whereas* others prefer to allocate more funds to marketing.
Whereas some businesses invest heavily in researching new products, others prefer to allocate more funds to marketing.

Exercise 2

1 It is a well-known fact that conservation projects can be costly. Nevertheless, they need to be prioritised.

2 Although some parents believe in the benefits of home tutoring, most think that children require the school environment for the full development of their social skills.

3 In spite of the warnings given by the medical profession, people still smoke.

In spite of the fact that the medical profession give warnings, people still smoke.
In spite of receiving warnings from the medical profession, people still smoke.

4 Social networking sites were designed to develop new friendships. However, their main use has been to communicate within existing peer groups.
Social networking sites were designed to develop new friendships. Their main use, however, has been to communicate with existing peer groups.

5 Whilst most film festivals in the world show one or two German movies, films 'Made in Germany' are not given the recognition they deserve.

27 Linking: adding

Exercise 1

1 Raw materials are becoming more expensive. In addition, the fuel costs involved in transporting them are increasing.

2 Besides improving staff performance, staff development opportunities tend to increase employees' loyalty to the company.

3 Not only is Sealtrack winning contracts in the private sector, it is also bidding successfully for major projects in the public sector.

4 A new recruitment process was introduced, with impressive results.

5 Changing the layout of the factory would be very expensive. It could, furthermore, delay production for several months.

6 Having so far done most of their business in the UK, Sealtrack is now developing products for the American market as well.

Exercise 2

1 Not only was Fast Track Solutions declared bankrupt, but its CEO was also given a six-year prison sentence for fraud.

2 As well as making record profits in 2011, Welltech won an award for its staff development programme.

3 Sealtrack's braking system is the most technologically advanced on the market. Moreover, it is selling at the cheapest price at the moment.

4 Compro streamlined its management structure, with 52 middle managers being made redundant.

5 Grigson plc have increased their market share in the UK **in addition to** winning new contracts in Spain.

6 **Not only** did Welltech lower production costs at its factory, **but it also** improved quality.

28 Linking: causes

Exercise 1

1 Crime rates have risen in this part of the city, **which** is why so many residents have sold up and left.

2 **On account of** the fact that the museum and gallery ...

3 The increased power of the media to question and criticise may have brought **about** a lack of respect for politicians.

4 The research facility was closed because **of** serious concerns about its standards of health and safety.

5 One reason **for** an episode of hyperactivity in children may be the excessive consumption of sugar.

6 A number of basic errors were made due to **the fact that** no trained medical staff were present at the time. OR
A number of basic errors were made **due to no trained staff being present** at the time.

Exercise 2

1 Since many citizens are dissatisfied with the way in which lobbyists influence Government policy, there are often calls for reform.

2 One source of public concern is the possible use of genetic testing by insurance companies.

3 Some adolescents appear to suffer from headaches and anxiety due to their repeated poor performance in computer games.

4 On the grounds that they would affect their trade, local shopkeepers attacked the new parking charges. OR
Local shopkeepers attacked the new parking charges on the grounds that they would affect their trade,

5 Syms argues that a period of mental illness may be triggered by an apparently trivial event.

29 Linking: results

Exercise 1

1 Unemployment in the region was **so** high that the Government felt obliged to establish an enterprise zone.

2 The digital revolution in broadcast media has led **to** a much wider range of programme choice for the consumer.

3 Accidents in laboratories may result **from** a lack of supervision.

4 Funding for the arts fell. **Therefore**, many groups and organisations were unable to continue.

5 Employment opportunities in the sector fell, **resulting** in increased competition for jobs.

6 Dickens regularly gave talks and readings, thereby **increasing** his fame with the public.

Exercise 2

1 Investment in small-scale technology such as mobile phone masts (has) resulted in considerable economic growth in the region.

2 Both of the town's electronics factories were forced to close during the recession. As a result, the only employment opportunities to be found are in the service and public sectors. OR
Both of the town's electronics factories were forced to close during the recession, as a result of which/with the result that the only employment opportunities to be found are in the service and public sectors. OR
Both of the town's electronics factories were forced to close during the recession and, as a result, the only employment opportunities to be found are in the service and public sectors.

3 The region was recovering from war. This meant that medicines were in short supply. OR
The region was recovering from war and this meant that medicines were in short supply.

4 Riots continued for ten days, which meant that many villages were left in ruins.

5 Radiation leaks at the Chernobyl plant resulted from the absence of a confinement shell.

6 Seasonal Affective Disorder (SAD) seems to stem from a shortage of sunlight.

30 Signposting

Exercise 1

1 preceding
2 latter, following
3 above
4 former

Exercise 2

1 In the paragraph **above**, we saw how Milan emerged as one of Italy's most important commercial centres.

2 After Paris, Lyon and Marseille are the second and third biggest cities in France **respectively**. OR
After Paris, Lyon and Marseille are, **respectively**, the second and third biggest cities in France.

3 By exploring the statistics in the table **below**, it will be possible to appreciate the scale of Germany's postwar recovery.

4 There is a certain amount of rivalry between Madrid and Barcelona. **The former** is the centre of power, while **the latter** often regards itself as the economic driving force of the country.

31 Using pronouns correctly

Exercise 1

1 Senior managers took their staff to a hotel, where **the managers/the former** gave presentations on possible future directions for the company.

2 To do **his or her** job well, a human resources manager needs imagination as well as knowledge of procedures. OR
To do their job well, human resources managers need imagination as well as knowledge of procedures.

3 The conference on performance management ended with a keynote speech. **The speech/ The latter** was a great success, according to those who attended.

4 A council of student representatives was formed at the university, and **its** task was to represent the views of the student body.

Exercise 2

1 warnings
2 trend
3 measures
4 phenomenon

Exercise 3

1 ... are based. **Those** who are most critical ...
2 ... despite warnings that such **a** measure ...
3 ✅
4 ... compared to **that** of a lottery.

32 Avoiding repetition of words

Exercise 1

1 Most young people make compromises with their parents that allow the family to work as an entity, but some teenagers seem unable to **do so/do this**.

2 The two housing trusts decided to merge in 2009. **Both** believed that working together would improve outcomes.

3 Of all the charities working with homeless people, the **one** whose name is most familiar to the public is Shelter.

4 There have been many attempts to renovate empty housing stock and make it available to families in need. The **latest** (one) has been sponsored by the property group Camden Holdings.

5 Stapleton Ltd agreed in 2006 to improve the living conditions of their 540 tenants in Islington, but when an inspection took place in 2008, it was evident that they had not **done so**.

Exercise 2 (sample answer)

The charity Homes for People invested some of their savings in a business with a scheme for contructing ecological housing on a site outside Leeds. The **location** for the **project** seemed ideal, but it became apparent after six months that very **few homes** were actually being **built**. When the charity contacted the **company** to establish why **half a year** had elapsed without any obvious progress, they discovered that the entire **venture** had been sub-contracted to a smaller **firm**.

33 Parallel structures

Exercise 1

1 to promote / deal with / monitor
2 have / know
3 an increase / a fall
4 meet / play / is
5 using / going through
6 plan / do not have

Exercise 2

1 The course syllabus includes **an analysis of** the concept of innovation, **the design/ designing of** technical images and **the preparation of** project specifications.

2 The music entitled 'Before Dawn' **was written** by Dominique Ferris and **published** in 2010.

3 The research will investigate the number of people **leaving** school early and **getting** married.

4 Equipment **has to be bought**, laboratories **set up** and **staff hired** before any work can begin.
5 Global air travel is **safe**, **convenient** and more **fuel-efficient** than it used to be.
6 When you entertain someone from another country, it's hard to decide whether to **shake** their hand or **wait and see** what they do first.

Exercise 3 (sample answers)

1 Teamwork is beneficial because it involves **mixing** with different types of people, **pooling** ideas and **reaching** joint decisions.
2 A successful marketing strategy needs **clear objectives, a wide-ranging advertising campaign** and **strong public support**.

34 Participles

Exercise 1

1 ❌ ('a new model' is not the subject of 'spotting)
2 ✅
3 ❌ ('he' is not the subject of 'written').
4 ✅
5 ❌ ('the proposed merger' is not the subject of 'sought')
6 ✅

Exercise 2 (sample answers)

1 **Having carried out** extensive market research, they launched the new product. / They carried out market research before **launching** the new product.
2 **Wishing** to streamline the operation, the management reduced staffing.
3 **Overtaken/having been overtaken** by competitors in terms of market share, the company had to respond quickly.
4 The garage, **experiencing** keen competition from other companies, began to struggle.
5 **Having drawn up** a shortlist of candidates, the officers passed it to the manager for review.
6 Customer satisfaction, **monitored** by in-store complaints records, rose to an all time high during the holiday period.

Exercise 3 (sample answers)

1 **Having lost** market share, Jagger plc made 100 staff redundant. **Operating** as a smaller company, it returned to profitability.
2 Bull Construction Ltd, **founded** in 2008, grew quickly. **Having landed** a major public sector

contract in 2009, the company moved to new premises.

35 Incomplete sentences

Exercise 1

1 ❌
2 ✅
3 ✅
4 ❌
5 ❌
6 ✅

Exercise 2 (sample answers)

1 All sentences apart from the first one should be underlined.
The jury system is a central plank of the British legal system. **However, there are** a number of critics of it who say that it is outdated **and that** many cases are too complex for ordinary members of the public. **As a result**, they feel that juries should not be used any longer.
2 The first and last sentences should be underlined.
There are a number of reasons why the ruling party might lose the next election **and** the state of the economy is probably the top one. **As** many people are losing their jobs and businesses are unable to attract investment, **there is** a growing loss of faith in the government.
3 The last two sentences should be underlined.
A backbench MP can rise to prominence **if** he or she makes an exceptional speech **which** is reported in the press or chairs a committee, particularly when **it** interviews public figures.
4 All sentences apart from the first one should be underlined.
TV watchers could not believe how many people the protest attracted **despite the fact that it was** one of the wettest days of the year. On every street in the city centre there were hundreds of protestors, **carrying** slogans and **denouncing** the government's policies.
5 The final sentence should be underlined.
Some politicians have become very rich after holding office **because** they have been appointed to company boards. The high profile they acquired while in office **also**

means that they can command high fees for lectures.

36 Avoiding long and disorganised sentences

Exercise 1 (sample answers)

1 Studies of youth culture in Britain always tend to focus on the 1960s as that is the period when many changes were clearly visible in British society and when the whole subject became a matter of public debate. **However,** many of these developments actually began in the 1950s and any study of youth culture should really begin in that decade.

2 Any study of international relations will show that alliances are constantly shifting so that nations who are close allies for a period of time can become enemies when circumstances change. **The reason why** some wars start **is that** a nation's interests have changed and to act in those interests they now oppose a political leader they previously supported.

3 The difference between sociological and journalistic approaches to events is that in the first approach sociologists have to use scientific methods to gather their information. Journalists, **on the other hand**, can easily make up information without witnessing the actual event, which sometimes makes them biased.

4 Prime Ministers are like senior managers in that they can delegate much of their power to individual departments, focusing their energy on overall strategy and presentation. **Another approach is that** they can micro-manage the individual decisions of their department heads, but if they choose this route, they risk being overwhelmed by the sheer scale of modern government.

Exercise 2 (sample answers)

1 ✅

2 George Orwell is chiefly known for his novels 'Animal Farm' and '1984' and these are still widely read today. **In addition**, he wrote a great deal of important journalism, for example 'Road to Wigan Pier' about the life of miners and the relevance of socialism.

3 ✅

4 It has been argued, with the benefit of graphic anecdotes, that organisations are hampered by health and safety legislation. **However,**

when individual elements of the law are closely examined, it becomes clear that it is an exaggerated interpretation by managers that is causing the problem, rather than the code itself.

37 When to use short sentences

Exercise 1 (sample answers)

1 Much of the housing in east London had been destroyed in the war and much of what remained could be categorised as slums. **Something had to be done.** Therefore a policy of rebuilding in the affected areas was devised and this involved the creation of many high-rise estates.

2 **Under the 1947 law owners no longer had full rights over their land.** Final permission for development instead passed to local authorities who were given powers not only to approve new proposals, but also to 'list' buildings of architectural interest, and thus protect them permanently from development.

3 New buildings can contrast significantly with the landscape around them, providing an interesting element of shock value, or they may blend in harmoniously, so that their presence is hardly noticed. **They must, however, take their surroundings into full account.**

Exercise 2 (sample answer)

As the building programme in many British cities continued in the 1950s and 1960s, opinions as to its effects differed. There were many who felt that it represented a necessary improvement, raising the standards of living of a great many people and transforming these cities into modern ones worthy of the modern age. **Other people were far less enthusiastic. These included many of the people actually living in this new housing.** They felt that it had been created by people who would never have to live in it and who had little or no knowledge of how their theories would impact on the residents.

38 Avoiding too many short sentences

Exercise 1 (sample answers)

1 The silent film era, **which** began in the late 19th century, continued until the 1920s **when** recorded sound became possible.

2   Politicians have become more and more
    reliant on focus groups, **which** came into
    existence in the 1990s **and** involve **carefully
    selected groups** of people giving their views
    on political issues.
3   Large hospitals can be cost-effective
    by moving staff members **who** are
    underemployed in their part of the building to
    an area of greater need.
4   A small restaurant **that** has ambitions to
    expand may decide to make an offer on
    adjacent premises **and in** this way it gains the
    additional space it requires.
5   The research team, **initially criticised** for
    making slow progress, was actually involved in
    a fundamental re-thinking of domestic heating
    systems, **which** would lead to an innovative
    and successful design.

Exercise 2 (sample answers)

1   The Industrial Revolution, **which** transformed
    the entire world, could be said to have started
    in Derbyshire and Shropshire, two adjacent
    counties in the north Midlands. Arkwright's
    Wheel, **which** used water power for the
    spinning of cotton, was invented in Derbyshire
    in 1771 **and** The Iron Bridge in Shropshire,
    built in 1781, was the first arch bridge made
    of cast iron.
2   Michael Cimino submitted a script for
    'Heaven's Gate', **then called** 'The Johnson
    County War', to United Artists in 1971. **Failing**
    to attract attract high-profile actors, the
    project was shelved until 1979, **when** it began
    shooting with a budget of $11.6 million,
    which had risen to $30 million by the time it
    was finished.

39   Building successful long sentences

Exercise (sample answers)

1   Sports psychology is based on the belief **that**
    many top competitors are of similar ability
    and **that** what separates winners from losers
    is their state of mind **and** their ability to meet
    the mental challenge as well as the physical
    one.
2   The 1990s was a very significant period in
    terms of the country's development, **as** its
    economy grew at a faster rate than ever
    before and there were **also** a number of social
    changes, **which** resulted in various problems.

3   Files stored long term on computers are easy
    to access and require little storage space, **but**
    there is a danger that, years or even decades
    later, the data may be unreadable by a
    malfunctioning machine **for which** spare parts
    are no longer available.

40   Generalising

Exercise 1 (sample answers)

1   Obesity **tends to be** the result of over-eating.
    Obesity is, **in general**, the result of over-
    eating.
2   **Most / The majority of** parents immunise
    their children against childhood diseases.
    Parents **tend to** immunise their children
    against childhood diseases.
3   ✅
4   **By and large**, children eat more junk food
    nowadays than they did in the past.
    Children **have a tendency to** eat more junk
    food nowadays than they did in the past.
5   ✅
6   ✅

Exercise 2

1   There is concern that antibiotics **are tending
    to** lose their effectiveness.
2   Attempts to educate the public about the
    need to adopt healthier lifestyles have, **in
    general terms**, been successful.
    In general terms, attempts to educate the
    public about the need to adopt healthier
    lifestyles have been successful.
3   **On the whole**, the system of health care
    currently in operation works well.
    The system of health care currently in
    operation works well **on the whole**.
4   Patients **have a tendency to** trust their
    doctors' opinions.
5   Children suffer from more coughs and colds,
    in general, than adults.
    In general, children suffer from more coughs
    and colds than adults.
    Children, **in general**, suffer from more coughs
    and colds than adults.
6   Experts were surprised that, **in most cases**,
    the treatment failed to work.
    Experts were surprised that the treatment
    failed to work **in most cases**.
7   The trial report noted that the tablets relieved
    the majority of symptoms.

8 People who exercise **tend not to** get ill as often as people who have sedentary lifestyles.

Exercise 3

When antibiotics were first developed, they completely changed the face of medicine. Illnesses that **tended to** be fatal, could suddenly be cured with a simple course of pills. Unfortunately, the long-term outcome has been that, **in general**, people over-rely on them and doctors over-prescribe them. What does this mean for the future? Unless scientists continue to produce new antibiotics, the ones we depend on today will, **in many cases**, no longer be effective.

41 Qualifying a statement

Exercise 1

1 The public health campaign was successful to the extent that it raised awareness of the issue. / To the extent that it raised awareness of the issue, the public health campaign was successful.
2 The treatment was effective insofar as it alleviated some of the symptoms for a period of time. / Insofar as it alleviated some of the symptoms for a period of time, the treatment was effective.
3 Exercise is important in that it can, according to research, facilitate mental health. / In that it can, according to research, facilitate mental health, exercise is important.
4 The advertising campaign worked in the sense that it removed some of the stigma attached to sexually-transmitted diseases. / In the sense that it removed some of the stigma attached to sexually-transmitted diseases, the advertising campaign worked.

Exercise 2

1 People who take no exercise and eat a great deal of junk food are likely to become obese.
2 Patients seem to require years of support to recover fully from post-traumatic stress disorder.
3 It is (highly) probable that high levels of stress at work will lead to illness.
4 Alcohol abuse appears to play a significant part in domestic violence. / It appears that alcohol abuse plays a significant part in domestic violence.

5 Drug rehabilitation schemes have, to some extent, reduced levels of addiction in inner-city areas. / Drug rehabilitation schemes have reduced levels of addiction in inner-city areas, to some extent.

Exercise 3 (sample answer)

The latest research **seems to indicate** that poor diet is a contributing factor in a number of serious illnesses. **It could be argued that** the Government should therefore increase the amount of money it spends on education programmes. Improving the nation's diet **is likely to** prove cost effective in terms of the money it will save the National Health Service. **There is** also **a (strong) possibility** that a better diet will lead to fewer people being ill at work, thus representing a significant saving to business.

42 Giving a definition

Exercise 1 (sample answers)

1 An avatar **is/was** defined by Spinrad in 'Songs from the Stars' (1980) as a …
2 A digital immigrant is a person **who** was born before the start of the digital age.
3 Data mining is a process **by which/whereby** a company develops profiles …
4 A computer virus is a destructive program **that can reproduce itself and be transmitted between computers**. (The Conficker worm is an example, not a definition.)
5 Apple Inc. **is an American corporation that** produces and sells consumer electronics, personal computers and computer software.
6 A mouse is a **device** for controlling the movement of a cursor on a computer screen.

Exercise 2 (sample answers)

1 Cyber bullying describes the use of online facilities to torment specific individuals.
2 Wikipedia is an online encyclopedia whose entries are written by volunteers.
3 Globalisation could be defined as the process whereby international financial and cultural systems become more uniform.
4 A USB flash drive is a device for storing data separately from a personal computer.
5 A chat room is an online forum that allows a group of participants to communicate with each other in real time.

43 Introducing an example

Exercise 1

1 how difficult it can be to pump groundwater
2 A range of educational activities
3 complications
4 laws ... designed to protect waterways ... from degradation
5 approaches to enhancing crop performance

Exercise 2 Sample answers

1 This can improve many people's quality of life by, *for example*, enabling them to have a better diet.
2 There are many ways to protect plants. Take for example, *the use of* pesticides. (Pesticides are not a 'way'.)
3 i.e. should be e.g.
4 Some statistics on organic farming can be surprising, for example, *those related to* sugar cane. (Sugar cane is not a statistic.)
5 ✅
6 ✅

Exercise 3

1 example (not illustration)
2 Take
3 such
4 illustrated
5 An / One

44 Citing

Exercise 1

1 As Jennings *states:* 'The home is of paramount importance because this is where a child's most basic needs must be met.'
2 No one really knew what term to use, until Mo (1995) *came* up with the expression, 'blue hour'.
3 ✅
4 Barton (2008) *says / points out / notes etc.* that few people really understand the problem.
5 Green *et al. argue* that price is always a factor.
6 ✅
7 ✅
8 According to Pine-Smith (1975) ~~argues~~, 'we have to take into account the child's home environment'.

Exercise 2

1 ✅
2 Compliance is a critical factor (Peters 2003; Lilley 1999).

3 ✅
4 While nobody can challenge this idea, 'other areas of a child's life also play their part' (Fielding 2004).
5 Grahams (2006) insists that 'this old notion has to be rejected once and for all'.

45 Incorporating data

Exercise 1

1 conducted
2 analysed
3 differences
4 significant
5 expectations
6 consistent
7 findings
8 reached

Exercise 2

1 eight percent / per cent
2 amount
3 250
4 number

Exercise 3

1 participants
2 conducted
3 aim
4 predicted
5 difference
6 variation
7 results
8 observations
9 finding

46 Paraphrasing

Exercise 1 (sample answers)

1 must/have to; open-mindedness/ broad-mindedness/understanding
2 condemned/denounced; cruel/inhuman/brutal
3 legislation/regulations; stop/halt; enthusiastically/unreservedly
4 energetically/vigorously; harmful/deleterious

Exercise 2 (sample answers)

1 The report advised the charity to make the range of its projects more extensive.
2 'Compassion fatigue' can result from an excess of disaster campaigns.
3 It is essential that aid workers are familiar with local customs.

4 Despite raising enough money, FoodAid was unable to get supplies to the region.

5 Aid workers on the ground need to respond creatively to unexpected situations.

Exercise 3 (sample answers)

1 Myers (2009) argues that the success of an aid advertisement depends on providing the public with key facts on the local situation as well as arousing sympathy.

2 According to Davis (2010), the Government will probably maintain its international aid spending despite its efforts to reduce the deficit.

3 Briggs (2011) notes that charities are currently competing more intensely than ever for public sympathy.

47 Formal language 1

Exercise 1 (sample answers)

1 One **advertisement** in a successful campaign shows a young **father** in a park, looking after **two children**, and failing to notice some of the dangers present in the situation.

2 In the promotion of their food products, some companies **seem to ignore** the health risks posed to young children.

3 Encouraging young people in the notion that it is **socially acceptable** to become drunk is **morally questionable**.

4 If young people suspect that they are to become the subject of a lecture, they may **make every effort to** avoid the campaign message.

5 Ronson points out that sedentary lifestyles can be found as often amongst **office workers** as within the home. OR as often **in the office environment** as …

6 The problem of overeating **will not be resolved** by health campaigns on their own. OR will not be resolved solely by health campaigns.

Exercise 2 (sample answers)

1 There is a persuasive argument for banning food and drink advertisements that target children under ten.

2 It has to be recognised that that cars play an important role in a person's sense of autonomy.

3 It seems preferable for the food industry to regulate itself in the area of advertising, rather than for new laws to be created.

4 There has been a greater demand amongst consumers for information about the food and drink that they purchase.

5 It must be remembered that the costs of treating the illnesses brought about by unhealthy lifestyles are shared by the whole of society. OR It should not be forgotten that …

6 There can be little doubt that young people are now much more aware of the dangers of alcohol abuse. OR It seems clear that …

48 Formal language 2

Exercise 1

1 An enquiry has been initiated into (the) voting irregularities that seem to have occurred in the north of the region.

2 A brief consultation took place between the President and the leader of the majority party, before the latter was pronounced Prime Minister. OR After a brief consultation between the President and the leader of the majority party, the latter was pronounced Prime Minister.

3 A series of laws was enacted to grant religious freedom to the population.

4 Monitors had to ensure that polling stations were accessible to all the adults in the region.

Exercise 2

1 successfully **addressed** the major problems …

2 … the army's **overwhelming** weaponry.

3 A **de facto** leader …

4 political freedom and **vice versa**.

5 … resulting in a **pro rata** reduction …

49 The language of argument

Exercise 1 (sample answer)

This essay will start by defining the term 'globalisation'. Next it will consider some of the drawbacks of this process in the developing world, and examine claims that globalisation brings about a loss of cultural identity. In the second half, the essay will describe some political gains that international integration may have assisted, and explore the recent success of a number of international campaigns. Finally, it will conclude that, on balance, globalisation has helped rather than hindered mankind.

Exercise 2

1 It can be **argued** that ...
2 A further objection **to** economic globalisation ...
3 The first point to be **made** is that ...
4 **Although** some aspects ...
5 Studies have **shown** that views ...
6 It follows that **there** is ...

50 Adjectives & adverbs

Exercise 1

This was <u>definitely</u> the beginning of a new era. Specially formed labels within the major record companies, catering for niche markets that were <u>continually</u> appearing, became the norm. People who enthusiastically followed styles of music that had previously been very much minority interests now found that the records they wanted to buy were <u>readily</u> available in shops. <u>Inevitably</u>, there were parallel developments in radio. Shows catering exclusively for these individual styles of music suddenly sprang up, and these rapidly acquired dedicated listeners, who <u>immediately</u> went out and bought the records they heard on the shows.

Exercise 2

1 ✗ incredibly
2 ✗ similarly
3 ✓
4 ✓
5 ✗ desperate
6 ✗ very

Exercise 3

1 Astonishingly, nobody had noticed this problem before. / Nobody, astonishingly, had noticed this problem before.
2 Similar research was going on elsewhere, coincidentally. / Coincidentally, similar research was going on elsewhere.
3 Unfortunately, nobody foresaw this problem. / Nobody foresaw this problem, unfortunately.
4 Obviously, no firm conclusions can be drawn from such little evidence. / No firm conclusions can be drawn from such little evidence, obviously.
5 Apparently/Seemingly, nothing could have been done to prevent the accident. / Nothing could have been done to prevent the accident, apparently/seemingly.

51 Using prepositions 1

Exercise 1

1 about/over, of
2 of, in, with
3 with, of
4 in, on
5 for, to

Exercise 2

1 Everything seemed to point *to the fact that* they were going to lose their funding.
2 ✓
3 The department had to deal with the repercussions of *assigning/the fact that they had assigned* difficult projects to junior staff.
4 ✓

Exercise 3

1 This is the area about which we have most knowledge.
2 Here are the results on which I based my assessment.
3 The survey identified individuals for whom there is no current provision.
4 You need to look at the groups into which the insects have been classified.
5 Sometimes there are problems for which we do not have explanations.
6 It turned out to be a situation from which most people benefited.

52 Using prepositions 2

Exercise 1

1 found
2 to
3 apart from
4 research
5 consists of
6 in

Exercise 2

1 regard
2 keeping / line
3 view
4 account
5 retrospect
6 terms
7 exception
8 light

Exercise 3

1 I would like to place emphasis on these aspects.
2 A postponement is in order, in view of the changes to the schedule.
3 We need to have a discussion about some of the conclusions.
4 Certain features were highlighted by the sombre background.

53 Using longer words

Exercise 1

1 likelihood, uncertainty, strengthened, strengthens, expansion
2 contributor, environmental, unstoppable
3 assessment, outdated, under-perform
4 probability, technological, transformation
5 characterised, disappointingly, unimaginative, leadership

Exercise 2 (sample answer)

There was **disagreement** among people as to which course of action would be the most **effective**. The company's founders felt **passionately** that their position was the correct one and they were **unsympathetic** towards the views of others. This **exemplifies** the kind of struggle going on within many organisations at the time.

Exercise 3

1 disheartening
2 illogical
3 unjustifiable
4 underestimate
5 inconceivable
6 non-compliant
7 irrespective
8 disorderly
9 inconsistent
10 unnatural
11 illegal
12 impure

54 Using single words for impact

Exercise 1

1 Undoubtedly
2 incomprehensible
3 misunderstood
4 immeasurable

Exercise 2

1 variable
2 highlighted
3 infrastructure
4 bankruptcy/bankruptcies
5 Inflationary
6 referendum

Exercise 3 (sample answers)

1 It is a (highly) competitive sector.
2 Many small businesses have computerised their stock-taking.
3 Innovation is crucial even for a well-established company.
4 Staff can become demotivated if managers fail to communicate.
5 The company was allegedly in breach of health and safety laws.

55 Phrasal verbs

Exercise 1 (sample answers)

1 It may take a small business more than a year to **recover from** a quarterly fall in sales.
2 During the train strike, Enco plc **provided** a special bus service to take employees from the factory to the head office.
3 A tier of middle managers were **made redundant**, and six junior staff were appointed to replace them.
4 If the pressure becomes too acute, a manager may be tempted to **resign from** his job.
5 In times of recession, companies often **reduce** the number of seasonal and temporary staff.
6 Some consumers are likely to feel they are being **exploited/cheated** if the monthly cost of calls rises dramatically after the trial period.
7 **Communicating** your ideas in a concise way is the key to success in a presentation.
8 A meeting was called in an attempt to **resolve** the dispute.

Exercise 2

1 Stevens argued that a committee should be **set up** to consider new ways of protecting the users of social network sites from online bullying.
2 Some whistleblowers will **speak out** even when their jobs are clearly at risk.

3 According to Sorelson, the final report did not **allow for** the possibility that some of the evidence may have been contaminated.
4 After **weighing up** the merits of both arguments, Polson concludes that further legislation did not offer a satisfactory way forward.
5 Barker **drew on** her experience in Kenya to argue for an international summit on the regulations governing the hunting of tigers.
6 The study **points up** the need for further research.
7 Several prominent figures **called for** the Minister's resignation. OR Several prominent figures called for/on the Minister to resign.
8 Errors in their statistics meant that their argument **did not hold up**.

56 Commonly misused words

Exercise 1

1 emigrants
2 imminent
3 assured
4 lose
5 infer
6 economic
7 complimentary
8 is composed

Exercise 2

1 incident
2 elicit
3 ensure
4 advice
5 effect
6 averse
7 apprised
8 historic

57 Commonly confused words – homonyms

Exercise 1

1 principle
2 too costly
3 ✅
4 allowed

5 passed
6 ✅
7 whether
8 bear

Exercise 2

1 your paying – you are paying
2 whose receiving – who is receiving
3 their trustworthy – they are trustworthy
4 its impossible – it's impossible
5 wether – whether
6 whose been – who has been
7 you're faith – your faith
8 their as – there as
9 there game – their game
10 it's advantages – its advantages

58 Key spelling rules

Exercise 1

1	controlling	control ends in vowel + 'l' so final consonant should be doubled
2	diaries	diary ends in 'y' so change to 'ie' when making plural
3	misquoted	quoted does not begin with 's' so letter should be singular
4	hygienic	the suffix is '-ic' so final 'e' is dropped
5	delightful	the suffix '-ful' never has double 'l'
6	irregular	'ir-' prefix requires double 'r'
7	biddable	'bid' is a word ending vowel + consonant so the final consonant should be doubled before the suffix is added
8	disappointed	in this case, no double letter with 'dis-' prefix

Exercise 2

1 openness / improvement
2 primarily / stressful
3 co-operation / noticeable
4 arguments / misconstrued
5 setting / achievement
6 continuities / awaiting
7 companies / prohibited
8 behaviour / dissimilar

59 Common spelling mistakes

Exercise 1

1	weird	6	opportunities
2	necessary	7	✔
3	committment	8	✔
4	✔	9	successful
5	stabilise	10	conceive

Exercise 2

Corrections
accomplished
religious
contemporaries
realities
knowledge
primarily
characters
portray
pessimistic

60 Writing an email to your tutor (sample answers)

Use correct grammar

Subject: Request for extension, Tony Hill, Social Studies, 2036

I'm really sorry but I'll be late handing in my assignment on care of the elderly. The due date's **the** 27th of this month and I know I **should have** finished by then but I wonder if I **can/ could** hand it in a week later. I've been off sick with a really bad throat infection and **haven't had** time to do all the reading yet. I'd like to ask for a week's extension, **which** would give me time to catch up. I hope my term grades **aren't** affected by this.

Punctuate your email

I've just started the module on **World** Archaeology (3033) and am finding the topic a bit too broad. I realise that, although I like the global coverage of the module, I would be better suited to something more specific. **As** I've always

had an interest in African Archaeology, could I change to this module?

Make clear connections within sentences

Subject: Sponsorship – Mongol Rally – Dave Couch

I've decided to take part in the Mongol Rally next year, **which** involves driving a car from Europe to Mongolia over the summer vacation. I wonder if you could sponsor me for **this event/activity?** It's not a race and I'm not trying to win anything – **it's** all about making it to the end of the route and donating your vehicle to a local charity. I've always admired **those** people who take on a charitable cause, so I've decided to have a go at **it/one** myself. Can I count on your support?

Make sure your sentences can be understood

I'd like to change the topic for my presentation. I did say that I would do it on communication issues, **having previously worked** on this. But I've found it very hard to find enough material or **get** the right ideas. Now I think I have a better idea that I've been working on. **Is it** ok if I do it on sensory deprivation instead?

Make sure style and function are appropriate

Subject: Re our appointment

I've just realised that I should have been in a meeting with you this morning! I **don't know** why I forgot but **I'm really sorry about it.** I'd like to re-schedule the meeting if possible **because** I still have some problems with my presentation. **Would Friday at 10 be possible**?

Use appropriate words and correct spelling

I've just applied for a job as a volunteer in a charity shop and I need to provide the names of two people who know me but who aren't relatives. I'd really **appreciate** it if I could put **your** name down as a **referee**. I think they'll contact you and it only **involves** writing a short paragraph about me, outlining my skills and giving some information about my **character**. I don't think there's any **point in** writing a lot as it's only a **temporary** job.

Could I also contact you for **advice** if I get an interview?

Index

References are to page numbers.
Entries in *italic type* indicate words or phrases whose use is illustrated and explained.
Numbers in **bold type** indicate pages on which the indexed grammatical term is a main topic.